WITHDRAWN

CROSSROADS

Also by Mark Radcliffe

Non-fiction
Reelin' in the Years
Thank You for the Days
Showbusiness

Fiction
Northern Sky

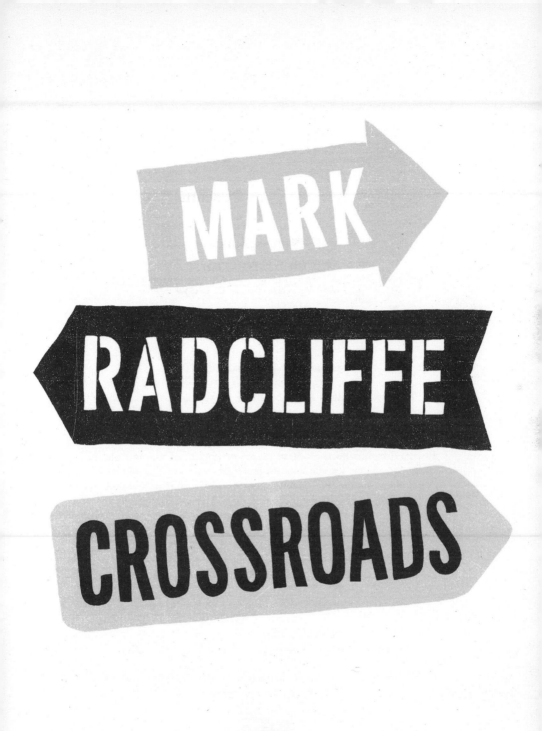

MARK RADCLIFFE

CROSSROADS

CANONGATE

First published in Great Britain in 2019
by Canongate Books Ltd, 14 High Street, Edinburgh EH1 1TE

canongate.co.uk

1

British Library Cataloguing-in-Publication Data
A catalogue record for this book is available on
request from the British Library

ISBN 978 1 78689 815 9

Typeset in Sabon LT Std by
Palimpsest Book Production Ltd, Falkirk, Stirlingshire

Printed and bound in Great Britain by Clays Ltd, Elcograf S.p.A.

For Bella, in sickness and in health

Contents

Introduction

For me, 2018 was an eventful year. I turned sixty. My dad died. So did my faithful companion, Toto the cocker spaniel. Big changes were forced on me at work. And to top it all I was diagnosed with cancer of the tongue and throat, from which, mercifully, I am in remission.

Some good stuff happened too, of course. I had a great sixtieth birthday in Uzès. One of my daughters got engaged, another got into her first-choice university and the third did brilliantly well in her GCSEs. Nice one, girls.

Another highlight was a trip to the USA with two old friends who'd also reached the same significant birthday. During this trip I found myself standing at a famous crossroads, which I'll tell you all about in Chapter 1. It felt like a serendipitous place to be as I was already experiencing something of a crossroads year myself, and it called to mind something someone had once said to me.

Years ago, when making a programme about the incendiary and hugely influential Canvey Island rhythm and blues band Dr Feelgood, I talked to the veteran music journalist Charles Shaar Murray about the group. He opined that they had found themselves at a crossroads in British music where a lot of interesting things fed in and a lot of equally interesting things, not least punk, headed out. That idea had always stayed with me and, as I found myself at a turning point – both literally and metaphorically – I got to thinking about how many musicians had reached crossroads moments of their own where everything changed for them personally, but more crucially how these events reverberated beyond the personal, shifting the course of music and influencing generations of artists to come.

With this in mind, I've interpreted the concept of the crossroads in several different ways. There are intersections of cultural movements, times when artists experienced a major change in their own lives, where society's mores took a sudden lurch or where a seemingly random turn in musical experimentation created something almost by accident, which would come to be seen as a key moment in the development of popular music.

So, in this book I've charted a course through some of those moments – although I should say that I don't consider what's contained here as a definitive list. You might well think of plenty of others as you read it. It's not intended to be a textbook. Everything here is true as far as I've been reasonably able to check, but I haven't got bogged down in historical detail. Rather, I wanted to take the bones of each story and understand the feelings and emotions that resulted in the creation of records which, when released, changed things for ever. And, perhaps, in some way better to understand the crossroads that I found myself at last year.

Mark Radcliffe. Not at an actual crossroads but in a cul-de-sac in Cheshire. Halloween 2018.

1

I Went Down to the Crossroads

'So, have you guys been laid?'

We've all had interesting conversations with taxi drivers in our time but as an opening gambit this still came as a something of a surprise. The cabbie in question was a generously proportioned African American gentleman, memorably kitted out in a white and gold velour track suit, oversized and unlaced Timberland boots and a leather fedora. It's not often you feel underdressed when being picked up in a minicab, but this was certainly one of those rare occasions.

On the morning in question this voluble, lavishly attired roué was collecting me and my travelling companions Jamie and Phil from a hotel in downtown Memphis, where North Front Street crosses Jefferson Avenue, to take us out to Graceland as per the itinerary for our collective sixtieth birthday road trip. I checked the schedule again just to confirm that 'getting laid' hadn't been slipped in there as an optional extra by our travel agent Shannon. It seemed unlikely even though they do always tell you to read through all documentation, but there didn't appear to be any brothel vouchers in our travel pack.

It was rainy that day in Memphis. The Mississippi river, which in my mind was going to be a glistening mile-wide ribbon peppered with chugging paddle steamers from the decks of which distant straw-hatted relations of Tom Sawyer dispensed cheery waves, was a Lowry-esque Salfordian smudge of turgid grey traversed by weary goods locomotives hauling their endless chains of rusting containers all the way to Arkansas.

Being practical souls, the three of us had dressed for the weather and were sitting in the taxi in our firmly zipped and poppered cagoules, while our charmer of a chauffeur indulged in several minutes of sexually infused badinage and innuendo with the ample receptionist. Once he took the wheel you would have thought that one look at us would have told him that the answer to his question was only ever going to be in the negative. People in Memphis to 'get laid' probably don't pack cagoules, do they? On reflection it occurred to me that his enquiry wasn't actually restricted to the immediate locale. Perhaps he glanced at us and wondered whether we'd been laid ever. Again, the way we looked that day, a response in the affirmative was by no means a fore-gone conclusion.

As longtime buddies since university days, and music

nuts our whole lives, Phil, Jamie and I had always planned a trip to some of the key historical sights of the birth of rock and roll and R&B. Memphis has not only Graceland, but also the Sun and Stax studios and the blues joints of Beale Street with their neon hoardings and promise of honest sweaty bands and cheap liquor. Nashville has a similar strip for the cream of country bar bands on Broadway, the Grand Ole Opry and the Country Music Hall of Fame. For the journey between the two cities we'd opted to take a scenic route called the Natchez Trace Parkway which rolls through endless miles of woodland, dipping into Tennessee, Alabama and Mississippi and stopping amongst other places at Elvis's birthplace in Tupelo where the shotgun shack he was born in still stands on its original footings.

Before heading on the parkway to Tupelo, though, we detoured to Clarksdale, Mississippi. In many ways it is such a classic American 'small town' that at first you wonder if you haven't strayed onto a film set. Naturally the streets are on a grid pattern and none of the build-ings are above two or three storeys high. Cars park diagonally into the curb, every store and house has a bench on the stoop and puffs of dancing dust swirl with every rare breath of breeze. The walls are painted in bright oranges, pinks and turquoises, or at least they are colours that were bright once. Chipped, faded and heat ravaged, it looks like there hasn't been a reliable painter and decorator in town since the mid-Sixties.

But there is history here. There are clues in some of the shops. In a settlement this size in the UK you might expect to find a mini-mart, a pub, a grocer's or butcher's, maybe a newsagent's, a scented candle and mindfulness parlour, artisan beard waxer and, if you're very lucky, a Post Office. You wouldn't happen upon a saxophone outlet very often. But there's one in Clarksdale. It's painted puce with various bluesmen caricatured on the frontage and is called Deak's Mississippi Saxophones and Blues Emporium. The sign on the pavement outside advertises 'harmonica lessons, sales and service, live music, folk art, open harp surgery and cold beer'. Top man Deak. Which shopping experience isn't enriched by the offer of cold beer except for perhaps test-driving a new sports car or motorbike? Or buying a gun perhaps. None of these items seemed to be readily available in Clarksdale although there were two other musical instrument suppliers, several more purveyors of folk art and cold beer and a heroically graffiti-infested fairy-lit blues club and soul food café co-owned by Morgan Freeman called Ground Zero for reasons that evade me. Dining in places named after memorials to major terrorist incidents is not something that it's easy to do but I had catfish nevertheless. It just seemed the right thing to do somehow. It was nothing to write home about although I suppose that's exactly what I'm doing now.

So why is there such a musical presence in a one-horse town like Clarksdale? Well, it's because it can make a convincing case for being the very place where the blues itself began, or at least the Delta blues as opposed to the Chicago blues (the birthplace of which you can probably guess at). The Delta blues came first. It is the folk music of that landscape. These are primal screams of poverty and pain featuring, for the most part, voice, acoustic guitar and harmonica, and even a few hours in hundred-degree temperatures traversing that flattened, sweating topography is enough for you to begin to understand how that music came about. Chicago blues came a bit later and developed when many of the dab hands of Delta migrated to Illinois and discovered the electric guitar. Ironically the generally acknowledged first Delta blues recording, Freddie Spruell's 'Milk Cow Blues', was recorded in 1926 in . . . Chicago. So although the birth of the blues happened on the Delta not Chicago, *recorded* Delta blues was born in the Windy City. Of course pinning down the actual birthplace of the genre to one point on a map is well nigh impossible. There are many locations, notably the Dockery Cotton Plantation which stakes a claim, but at the heart of Clarksdale's bid is one of the greatest legends in all of rock and roll.

You come into Clarksdale on Highway 61. As this was my first time there, it felt inappropriate to soundtrack the drive with Bob Dylan's 'Highway 61 Revisited' but next time I'll be sure to put that right. Just before you hit town there's an intersection with Highway 49. It's a wide but nondescript junction with a Sonic petrol station and various stores offering hot food and tobacco. Traffic lights hang from scrawny electric cables above a central grass island. It's not particularly well tended, though there is a flower bed, and a utilitarian grey wiring box is mounted on a telegraph pole. It's a junction like hundreds of thousands of others in the USA. Except that it isn't.

Also rising from the turf is a post with three semi-acoustic guitars clinging to it and a sign under each of them that says 'The Crossroads'. For this is not a crossroads. It is *the* Crossroads. And, at that moment, having been experiencing major life changes myself it felt like a significant place to be. The whole trip was planned to celebrate our landmark birthdays, but it also served as a welcome escape from dealing with stuff back home, and standing on this spot seemed to bring all those feelings together. So what was it about this spot that made it such a symbol of change and transformation and one that altered the course of popular music?

Robert Johnson, or possibly Spencer, or one of around eight other surnames he adopted at various times, was born in Hazlehurst, Mississippi, in 1911. He was, like most black people in the States, from impoverished stock and raised in a town that was a real powerhouse for the growing of tomatoes and cabbages but had little else going for it, bearing in mind this was at least a century before the lilies were gilded and cabbage was labelled a superfood and tomatoes a fruit. Even had he known all of that, it seems unlikely that young Robert would have found the information fascinating enough to make him want to stick around. It's on the Delta. The soil is fertile. Stuff grows. So what? And so he became an itinerant musician and agricultural labourer, at one time ending up at the famed Dockery Cotton Plantation where the workforce at one time or another also included Delta blues legends Charley Patton and Howlin' Wolf.

Over the years that followed there were various recorded sightings of Johnson all over the region as he scraped a living singing in juke joints or on street corners. In Beauregard, Mississippi, he hooked up with Ike Zimmerman who famously practised his guitar-playing and singing in graveyards at night. In Robinsonville he spent some time with another giant of the scene Son House who seemed to take quite a shine to Robert and liked his harmonica playing (perhaps he'd had lessons at Deak's), but considered him a very poor guitarist and average singer.

It's clear that, not unlike our taxi driver, the young Robert Johnson was a dude with some presence. He was evidently a charismatic performer, if prone to wandering off when he got bored, and was effortlessly persuasive with the ladies. That Robert Johnson got laid, and regularly, is not in doubt. The cagoule wasn't launched until the early Sixties in the UK when former Royal Marine Noel Bibby registered the Peter Storm trademark. However, even if they had been available in Mississippi in the Thirties it seems unlikely that Robert would have bought one because he was a dapper guy. Nomadic he may well have been but in the only photos we have of him he was what blues aficionados ZZ Top might call a 'Sharp Dressed Man'. There are really only two portrait images that are generally seen. In one he has a cigarette hanging nonchalantly from his lip at a louche angle, as he shapes a barre chord in braces and a white shirt. In the other more famous picture, which is reproduced in a peeling mural on a Clarksdale gable end, he is resplendent in a pristine chalk-striped suit with pocket handkerchief, shirt, tie and a rakishly cocked trilby. His spindly fingers once again bestride the neck of the guitar he is most associated with, a Gibson L-1 archtop, the instrument which by rights should sit on The Crossroads marker post. He looks every inch the superstar, the Prince of his day, even though he would actually go higher up the ranks of the nobility by being dubbed 'The King of the Delta Blues'.

But hang on. If Son House was right and Johnson was a journeyman in terms of his guitar-playing abilities, then how did he reach these exalted heights?

Roughly four centuries before Robert Johnson's lifetime, in what is now Stuttgart, lived, legend has it, a scholar, magician and alchemist called Johann Georg Faust. A restless soul, he found himself as dissatisfied with the incantations and inculcations of the town of Knittlingen as Robert Johnson would come to be with the dubious fruits and over-hyped superfoods of Hazlehurst, and began to wonder if there was a way of deriving greater rewards and excitement from this earthly drudgery. This is a thought many of us have had and have sought to confront by buying a new sports car or motorbike, experimenting with an inadvisable wardrobe makeover, returning in late middle age to a foam party in a cavernous Ibizan disco-theque or getting laid by a younger consort. In fact, Faust did go down this latter route with a fragrant Fräulein by the name of Gretchen who would later be arrested for murder after drowning their son. So that went well. However, the key part of Faust's plan to negotiate the midlife crisis was to recruit a bit of help from the Devil.

Summarily summoning Mephistopheles, Faust made a pact to enjoy a bounteous and luxurious life on earth in return for letting his soul head off to Hell when it was all over. Given this came in his sixtieth year, this might not seem like a grand old age but remember this was Württemberg in the fifteenth century and so the equivalent today would be living until you were seven hundred and fifty. Probably.

Now, you might be wondering why Faust had need of Satanic assistance, being as he was already an alchemist and therefore presumably able to transmute base metal into gold. One would have thought that colossal material riches would automatically ensue from having that ability just as it does from being able to play football to Premiership standard nowadays. So why would he throw his soul onto the table as a bargaining chip? Perhaps he took a gamble that the Devil might not come back to collect his debt. This seems foolish, though to be fair we're still a couple of hundred years off the Brothers Grimm collecting the story of Rumpelstiltskin. If this cautionary, and indeed Germanic, tale had been available to Faust perhaps he would have thought again. These gargoyles of the underworld always come back to close the deal. Rumpelstiltskin was absolutely clear that if the miller's daughter wanted to marry the king then he would use his alchemical artistry to spin straw into gold as required, but he would be nipping back in the future to collect her first-born sprog as payment in full. Even then, he gave her a get-out clause. If she could guess his name then he would cancel said debt. And here it was that the titular imp made his crucial error. After two nights of name guessing (it's not Keith or Darren or Son House or Howlin' Wolf), he camps out in the woods and dances round his own campfire singing:

Tonight, tonight, my plans I make
Tomorrow, tomorrow, the baby I take
The queen will never win the game
For Rumpelstiltskin is my name.

Didn't he know he was in a fairy tale and there was bound to be a woodsman or hunter lurking nearby? Why if feeling the urge to sing didn't he choose one of many songs appropriate to a woodland setting such as 'A Forest' by The Cure, Hank Williams' 'Settin' the Woods on Fire' or 'I Talk to the Trees' as performed on the soundtrack to *Paint Your Wagon* by Clint Eastwood? And so of course he was overheard and the message relayed back to Her Majesty who promptly proclaimed his name and sent him on his way, making me think that he might not have been an incarnation of Lucifer but just a really gobby goblin, albeit with a handy side-line in precious metal transmogrification. And another thing, if you can already spin straw into gold then why not just do that and buy all the sports cars and motor-bikes you like without getting into a tangle at the palace?

I digress (often) and what, you may ask, does any of this have to do with Robert Johnson? Well, here's the thing. Though his precise movements are hard to track we do know he was married to a woman called Caletta Craft and in 1932 they were living in Clarksdale and approaching Robert's date with destiny. In a Faustian pact he is supposed to have encountered a massive, mesmerising black man at the Crossroads who agreed to show him lots of brilliant licks on the guitar and educate him in the art of killer songwriting in exchange, like our friend in Stuttgart, for his soul in perpetuity when the time came. You can understand the temptation: it is often said that the Devil has all the best tunes although I don't think he had 'Dancing Queen' or 'Get Lucky' so that might not be entirely accurate.

What's clear is that after this encounter, an alchemical reaction took place transmuting Johnson's base skills into blues gold (if that's not oxymoronic, colour-wise). Within a very short space of time, our itinerant harmonica-toting busker had made his classic recordings in 1936 and 1937, which include tellingly 'Me and the Devil Blues', and had become the Jimi Hendrix of his day. In fact Eric Clapton would later proclaim Robert Johnson as a prime influence. Unfortunately the deal went sour as I suppose a deal with the Devil is wont to do. Johnson died aged twenty-seven, perhaps the first legend to check out at that number on a list that also includes Hendrix, Amy Winehouse, Brian Jones, Jim Morrison, Kurt Cobain and Janis Joplin. Not only that but his recordings were unsuccessful during his short lifetime and only celebrated posthumously.

Yet those recordings did change things for ever. It's not just that they influenced so many other artists but they have also cemented rock and roll's association with the dark side. In Robert Johnson's time just singing secular songs was enough to find yourself accused of selling your soul to the Devil. You had strayed from the heavenly light into the cesspit of the shadows. Black is the colour of rock and roll. The night is the time of rock and roll. Godlessness, misbehaviour, overindulgence and debauchery are the pulse of rock and roll. Robert Johnson was the first man alive to realise that.

Now, there may be some of you who think that a lot of this is supposition and hearsay and in any case hinges on the existence of God and Satan. Fair enough, but look at the cast iron facts behind the myth. There was definitely a Robert Johnson. Or maybe Spencer. Or maybe another surname. He definitely died when he was twenty-seven in 1938, shot by the jealous husband of a ladyfriend he was escorting. Or possibly by drinking poisoned whiskey. Or by contracting incurable syphilis. No matter, he is buried at Mount Zion Missionary Baptist Church in Morgan City, Mississippi. Unless you prefer to visit his nearby gravestone at Payne Chapel, Quito. Tell you what, why not dip down to his headstone at Little Zion Church just north of Greenwood, then you've seen all three. Then again you might think, as some do, that he lies unmarked in a pauper's grave somewhere. What's beyond doubt though is that Robert Johnson met an extravagantly modish, darkly persuasive and mysterious figure at the Crossroads where Highways 61 and

49 cross. Unless you prefer the intersections of 1 and 8 at Rosedale, or 28 and 51 at Hazlehurst. Clearer than that I cannot be.

Unlike Robert Johnson, Phil, Jamie and I did not get laid in Clarksdale, Memphis, or anywhere else on that trip. Not that our enthusiastic taxi driver didn't tantalisingly hint that the knowledge at his disposal would certainly extend to the full range of personal services available in town.

'So, you guys been laid?'

'Errmm, no, we haven't.'

A beat.

'D'you guys wanna get laid?'

'Errmm, that's very kind, but no, thank you very much. How long does it take to get to Graceland?'

It only came to me months later. A charismatic black man in lavish attire had beckoned us towards a portal to an underworld of temptation and debauchery. Had we, like Robert Johnson, encountered the Devil at a crossroads? What, at that stage in my life, would be the ramifications if I had chosen to go a different way?

2

The Gates of Hell Opening

A thunderstorm rages. A solitary, solemn church bell echoes from across the marshlands. In front of a gently decaying water mill is a tendrilous and bedraggled autumnal garden where a lonesome crow perches on a mottled tree trunk and observes a young woman of deathly pallor dressed in black. Her expression is inscrutable. Okay, so far so familiar to anyone who has tried to organise a family holiday at a country cottage with a reluctant teenager going through a bit of a goth phase who has finally, after several warnings, had to be forcibly separated from her mobile phone.

But then what happens? Nearby (but out of view), in a dank storeroom lit only by candlelight (probably), three of the Four Horsemen of the Apocalypse begin to create a sound from just three notes that will change rock and roll. We may indeed have caught them in the greatest act of musical alchemy ever achieved: transmuting base metal not into mere gold, but heavy metal itself. Or at the very least Black Sabbath, for it is they, creating what the fourth horseman Ozzy Osbourne described as a noise 'like the gates of hell opening'.

I love Black Sabbath. Their 1971 classic *Master of Reality* was the first album I ever bought. I paid Pete Leatham at school one English pound for it, though my dad may have gone halves with me as I recall. Black Sabbath's debut eponymous album was released in 1970 followed by *Paranoid* later the same year, on the cover of which a dumpy hombre in a motor scooter helmet appears to be brandishing a plastic scimitar in some chilly and spartan woodland copse for no good reason. What a body of work they amassed in those early years. *Paranoid* also gave the band their breakthrough hit with the title track in which, rather unfairly and ungallantly I've always thought, Ozzy terminated a relationship with a lady because she couldn't help him with his mind. Helping Ozzy with his mental state would turn into a job requiring many different layers of expertise and understanding down the ensuing years, but unless some kind of demand for psychiatric assistance had been made clear to this unnamed Missy of the Midlands on the first or second date, I don't really think it was fair to expect it later on.

In 1972 came another classic album in *Vol. 4*, with tracks like 'Supernaut' nailing down a formula that would be slavishly imitated down the years though never equalled, with *Sabbath Bloody Sabbath* following in 1973. I would finally get to see them live on 24 May 1974 when they played at the Free Trade Hall in

Manchester supported by Black Oak Arkansas. I remember the day vividly. I had carefully rolled some earplugs out of cotton wool, cunningly stiffened with my own earwax to train the recalcitrant fibres into balls, and placed them in a small plastic box that once held lavender-scented sweets, in the bib pocket of my Brutus brushed denim dungarees. As me and my familiar assemblage of acne-ridden amigos were sitting in the cheapest seats in the upper circle this careful protection of hearing may have seemed overcautious but these were pre-health and safety times and gigs were loud. When The Who played Charlton Athletic's ground The Valley the week before I saw Sabbath, it was so loud that it could be heard in space having bounced off the Great Wall of China. Possibly. Look, things were LOUD, alright? If we went to a gig on a Saturday night and our ears weren't still ringing at school on Monday it hadn't been loud enough.

I suppose in many ways those were the musical rules that bound our particular gang together. Teenage fandom is by its very nature tribal and if you are going to experience seismic shifts in your musical discovery and appreciation that will stay with you all your life it seemed only right that these experiences should be collective. More than that, though, at the heart of this story lies one of the most crossroads moments in all of rock and roll – and it goes something like this.

The members of Birmingham band Earth tended to gather at the flat of bassist Terry 'Geezer' Butler, where the interior redecoration, presumably at the expense of a hefty deposit, had been heavily influenced by the under-ground's obsession with the occult. The counterculture was still shapeshifting after the Summer of Love in 1967 and explorations in how to open the doors of perception went in all kinds of directions including to some very dark recesses. The striking thing about all the various ways that were investigated to throw off the shackles of polite society is how they all came to the same conclusion that it could be done in one of three ways. First, by taking large quan-tities of mind-bending narcotics. Second, by having sexual liaisons with as many people as possible. And finally, by having sex with as many people as possible while simul-taneously taking large quantities of mind-bending narcotics. Led Zeppelin's Jimmy Page became mightily infatuated with the teachings and experiments of master of the dark arts Aleister Crowley, whose oft-quoted mantra chimed easily with the era's new-found freedom: 'Do what thou wilt shall be the whole of the Law.' Geezer Butler's interest in occultism and satanic ritual appears to have been consid-erably less intense than Jimmy Page's in consisting mainly of liberally slapping on the Crown matt black emulsion and stencilling a few upside-down crosses on the bedsit wall.

Opposite Geezer's gaff there happened to be a picture house and while the band were idly cogitating on that evening's likely doors of perception openings, Butler was struck by the regular queues of punters eager for the latest horror films. Sensing that all manifestations of the dark side seemed to make for good box office, and had cost him a few bob in decorating expenses, he decided that if they could shroud their work in a cloak of shadows they might be on to something. Taking their new name Black Sabbath from the title of a 1963 Boris Karloff film they were off. But what did a band called Black Sabbath sound like?

The important thing to remember with bands like Black Sabbath and Led Zeppelin is that they weren't strictly heavy metal bands to begin with. They were heavy blues bands, and in fact, although Sabbath may well have invented heavy metal (though the phrase first appears in the Steppenwolf anthem 'Born to be Wild'), all their initial inspiration came from the blues. The blues that came out of the Mississippi Delta was the folk music of the times while also laying down the foundations of rock and roll. It was folk music because it was the voice of the oppressed, overworked, underpaid working man and woman. But it was also rock and roll because this voice spoke with anger, force and aggression. There are tenets laid down in the Mississippi Delta blues that go through punk and beyond. The primal yelp of Muddy Waters, Robert Johnson and in particular Howlin' Wolf influenced generations of artists desperate to explode in the same way. Theirs is a real passion, fuelled by a life of backbreaking work in the cotton plantations.

Bands of the Sixties beat era could hardly claim to know the horrors of slavery. They did know poverty and working-class life, though, which, while hardly comparable, did come with their own set of hardships which found expression and outlet in the blues. All the bands of that period were backstreet kids looking for a way out. Okay, the Beatles' story had some semi-detached suburban mise en scène but the Stones, The Who, the Small Faces, The Animals, the Yardbirds, The Hollies and Gerry and the Pacemakers were all artful dodgers gazing at the stars. And pop stars of the Sixties were generally of humble beginnings. The label stalwarts of Tamla Motown were all drawn from the Detroit housing projects and Abdul 'Duke' Fakir of the Four Tops once talked of having a length of rope to hold his trousers up as he was unable to afford a belt.

Of course there are notable exceptions to this sweeping generalisation. Not all groups came from humble backgrounds. Genesis met at Surrey's uber-poshington Charterhouse School near Godalming. One of the accepted ways of writing new material in those days was to go to a barn, bothy or even water mill somewhere and 'get it together in the country'. Led Zeppelin and Traffic both tried this with considerable success. When Genesis decided to do the same thing, it was fortunate that the family of their road manager and schoolmate Richard Macphail had a cottage standing empty which they could take over free of charge. That was unlikely to happen to The Animals whose family homes had yet to have indoor lavatories. Phil Collins insists that when he went to said bucolic toff's Hobbit holiday home, he was greeted by bassist Mike Rutherford – who should surely be played by Bill Nighy in the biopic – wearing a smoking jacket, and not in irony. Certainly it seems like Mike Rutherford is not the kind of guy whose trousers have ever been kept up by rope.

In recent times much has been made of the rise of the middle-class pop star who has come to fame either through the BRIT School route, or with a certain amount of family money and security behind them. The theory is that young people are in so much debt early in life thanks to the insanity of the university fee and student loan system, and the cost of living in general, that taking a chance on jamming with your spoddy mates and hoping for a lucky break in the early stages of your earning capacity is just too risky. You might never catch up and be off the housing ladder for ever. It should be stated that genres such as grime do seem to have returned to a time of stars emerging from humble council estate backgrounds but the situation for bands has changed. In decades past, a group of wannabe rockers could just huddle together for warmth in a squat and travel the country in all weathers in a Commer FC van without an MOT but with a condemned sofa squeezed in behind the driver and shotgun seats. Seat belts? Don't be silly. Sign on the dole occasionally and you had all you needed to be a band and live slap bang in the middle of the pre-gentrified inner cities. That template held good for almost half a century but, thanks to the lack of affordable housing and artists no longer being able to colonise down-at-heel neighbourhoods, it can't happen now.

Looking back at the Seventies, it also seems to have been a time when even the trappings of success were themselves more modest than we might assume. Look at pictures of Mick Jagger at home in the early days of the Stones' fame. Though he was living in a small London flat, he had not one, but two Trimphones at his disposal. He had well and truly made it in a world where most households used a call box. A SodaStream? Utter decadence. Manifestations of wealth were not something that the working-class hero became afraid to brandish though. John Lennon may well have imagined no possessions, although he seemed to have plenty in his big white mansion, but try telling that to the Mods and the Teds who spent every penny they had on the sharpest duds in which to swagger about town. There are cautionary tales however. Geezer Butler once came back to the Midlands streets of his childhood in a new Rolls-Royce which, thanks to the handbrake not being fully engaged, duly cruised driverless down a steeply inclined grimy terraced street followed by the harassed and humbled hobgoblin of the bass whose pursuit was not especially aided by his precipitously high platform boots.

One of the things I've noticed in many years of conducting interviews is how down-to-earth and self-deprecating the rock idols of the West Midlands are. Grand viziers of glam Noddy Holder and Roy Wood have become dear friends of mine and are the cheeriest, breeziest company you can keep. I've had the pleasure of Sabbath guitarist Tony Iommi's company on several occasions and have found him to be polite, funny and fascinating. I met Justin Hayward of The Moody Blues at Glastonbury and found him to be as courtly an individual as I have ever met. I don't know Jeff Lynne but I'm reliably assured he's just the same despite having spent yonks hanging around with Bob Dylan, George

Harrison and Roy Orbison. Even Robert Plant, once the biggest, preeniest, bare-chested-est, luminescent mane-est rock god on the planet is a man who goes to watch Wolverhampton Wanderers and has an impish sense of humour. So why should that be?

It has been suggested that the geographical location of Birmingham leaves it without another rival city within spitting distance. I've spent most of my life in or near to Manchester, a town which has produced some of the music and bands I dearly love, but I couldn't honestly say that all the creators of that soundtrack have been grounded all-round good guys. This is in no small part due to having to be constantly on the watch for showers of sarcasm sailing up the M62 from Liverpool a mere thirty miles away. Like Castor and Pollux, our great northwestern metropoli are forever shackled together. It's the same for Leeds and Sheffield. And Glasgow and Edinburgh. Does constantly having to fight your corner against plucky local opposition put that chip on your shoulder? Or maybe Birmingham, sitting in the centre of the country, gave its denizens a more pragmatic view of life. North, south, east or west? Sometimes the cross-roads itself can prove the best.

Whether or not Sabbath's riffmeister general Tony Iommi feels a sense of gratitude to his manual labouring past is hard to say as an almost unique set of circum-stances almost ended his career at the very point it was due to begin. Iommi was the Birmingham-born son of parents from Palermo. A guitarist of some repute through working with bands like the Rockin' Chevrolets and the

Polka Tulk Blues Band, he had also had a stint in Jethro Tull. Having informed his family that he was leaving behind a steady job at the metalworks for a life on the road with his Sabbath soulmates he casually dropped into the conversation that, with that decision having being made, he wasn't bothering to go in for his last day. Mamma Iommi, with a work ethic drilled into her in the vineyards of Sicily, was having none of that and duly despatched her son to do the honourable thing and fulfil his last shift. Unfortunately once he got to work Tony was informed that due to some other less dutiful employee having failed to clock in, he would be working on a machine he'd never operated before: a guillotine press.

And so it was – and it feels like there ought to be a clatter of thunder at this point – that during his last day at work before leaving to become a professional guitarist, Tony Iommi duly guillotine pressed the middle two fingers of his right hand. And him a left-handed guitarist as well, meaning those were the very digits despatching the riffs from the fretboard. All that remained were fleshy stumps from which lengths of feeble-looking bone protruded and Iommi was, not unreasonably, informed by medics in casualty that he would never play the guitar again – or presumably operate a guillotine press.

The story might have ended there, were it not for the intervention of a foreman at the foundry who told the digitally challenged wunderkind about Django Reinhardt. Reinhardt, born in 1910, was a Belgian Romani gypsy jazz guitarist who played the best gypsy jazz guitar that has ever been played. On the road from a young age, he married in his teens and lived in a caravan with his wife Florine who eked a living making artificial flowers. One night on his way to bed, the unchained Django managed to stagger into a candle, upturning it and causing a tempestuous blaze to rip through their vardo – speeded on its way by the copious quantities of celluloid onboard to be used in his wife's labours. Reinhardt suffered extensive burns and narrowly missed out on having to have a leg amputated. The fourth and fifth fingers of his left hand were reduced to smouldering, useless stumps. And this, the opposite of Tony Iommi's situation, for a right-handed guitarist. Catastrophic. Like Tony, doctors told him he'd never play again yet Django refused to accept this prognosis and taught himself to play with the fingers he had left. In 1934 he formed the Quintette du Hot Club de France with legendary fiddle player Stéphane Grappelli and continued to play the greatest gypsy jazz guitar that has ever been played.

Inspired by Reinhardt's overcoming of adversity, Iommi began to think of ways he could tackle the business of holding down the guitar strings with his ravaged fingertips and began to experiment with some melted tops of Fairy Liquid bottles. Moulding them into shape, and eventually topping them with strips of a leather jacket, he began to achieve the right traction for shaping the chords. However, the tension on the strings meant it was a painful process, and certainly too tortuous to be endured throughout the length of a full set. And so, in the simplest possible way of reducing that tension, the strings were detuned to as many as three semitones below bottom E. And once he got down there, as Ozzy accurately noted, 'it sounded like the gates of hell opening'.

Iommi could so easily have taken a different exit from his own crossroads, but instead his accident made him decide to forge ahead, resulting in the creation of Sabbath's genre-defining sound: a sound that they would not otherwise have discovered. The *Black Sabbath* album was recorded at Regent Sound Studios in London on 16 October 1969 in a mere six hours. The band were not present at the mix as they were already en route in the van to another gig. They pretty much just put it down as they would have played it live and Geezer Butler is no doubt quite right when he says the sound of it has stood the test of time because it is so unadorned with any studio trickery of the day which would have dated so badly. Less is certainly more, although that particular cliché may still be one which Iommi, looking at his hands, finds hard to accept. Nevertheless it's true. Especially if you have more to begin with. When I listened to the album's title track recently I was astonished to notice – in the brutally simple guitar and bass notes combined with Bill Ward's uniquely hyperactive drumming – a distinct resemblance to tracks recorded by Joy Division nearly a decade later. Their music, too, had a dark heart in the lyrical pain of Ian Curtis.

And yet for all that, it is questionable whether Sabbath's music really does have a dark heart. If the

Sabs ever did have any real interest in the occult it seems that they soon grew bored of the Ouija board, instead taking large quantities of drugs and having sex with as many people as possible. But being essentially four lads from the backstreets of Brum they seem to have retained an inherent ordinariness, and certainly a sense of humour. I met the four of them once backstage at a radio programme I was broadcasting from the ill-fated UK Music Hall of Fame. During our chat Ozzy cheerfully admitted that yes, after a huge gig at the Milton Keynes Bowl while the band were taking the applause at the front of the stage, he did pull down Bill Ward's tracksuit bottoms as his fists were pumped ceremoniously aloft because 'he's got a big old schlong has Bill'. You've got to love that. There was no sign of Bill Ward's schlong, or indeed any other part of him, at the final Sabbath hometown show on 4 February 2017, and that seems to me a great shame. Even if unable to play the full show he should surely have had a part it in somewhere.

At the Manchester Free Trade Hall in 1974, even though Bill was behind the drums, I failed to glimpse the same appendage. But I did see Black Sabbath. And standing bombazine-clad and brooding, like the Count of Monte Cristo with a Gibson SG, at the heart of the band where he would be the only ever-present member for very nearly fifty years, was Tony Iommi. The man who, due to an accident with some heavy metal, invented heavy metal.

3

Disco Sucks!

Gloria Gaynor may not have considered herself to be one of pop's innovators, but her stellar performance on the 1978 anthem 'I Will Survive' helped to seal it in our hearts for ever. Its life-affirming message of self-reliance and stubborn independence empowered all genders, sexualities and races alike and confirmed that the new disco scene was the perfect manifestation of the multicultural society.

Most genres of music have their target audience, be it teenage girls or moody goths and, while it's possible that there are Rastafarian heavy metal fans out there, I've never come across one. Genres are, to a degree, tribal. But not disco. Disco welcomed one and all. You were invited to participate and no one would judge you. The insistence on fun at its core has also enabled many to dismiss it as not being a 'serious' musical strand and overlook the perfect pop that was created in its name, 'I Will Survive' being a notable example. Gloria found herself as one of the icons for the new inclusivity when she gave memorable voice to this celebrated song.

Disco, then, was a musical crossroads, where many different clans assembled, joined hands and embarked on a hedonistic journey together. So you'd think that meant it would have been viewed at the height of its popularity with unanimous positivity.

And yet if you had been ambling around Chicago on 12 July 1979 and had wound up at the crossroads of Shields Avenue and West 35th Street, you'd have been aware of crowds gathering. This was not in itself unusual as this intersection was the location of the Comiskey Park stadium and home of the Chicago White Sox major league baseball team. The team weren't always called the White Sox of course. Before that, they were the Chicago White Stockings which makes them sound more like an effete assemblage of Regency dandies than a rough and tough, wad-chewing bunch of hard-hitting hoodlums. Prior to that they were called the Sioux City Cornhuskers which is a terrific name for a team. It suggests that though the act of removing the husk from an ear of corn is no great boast in itself, these were guys used to long days out in the burning heat of the fields and weren't going to be dispatched lightly. And Sioux City let you know they were from the Old West, pioneers and frontiersmen who would look you in the eye, spit copiously into the dust, and casually thwack your best pitcher for a home run. For the Detroit Tigers arriving at the Comiskey Park stadium to play the White Sox on 12 July 1979, whether feeling the fear or not, they would soon be involved in one of the strangest musical and sporting events of all time.

Steve Dahl was a DJ on Chicago's local radio station WLUP-FM. Steve broadcasts to this day and I've heard him described as a shock jock, which I take to mean someone who makes inflammatory right-wing statements to offend an audience who can't be offended because they've tuned in knowing that they are going to agree with you. Anyway, let's say that Steve was a man of firmly entrenched views and one of the things he was dead set against was disco. The week before the Comiskey Park incident, and by then at a different radio station, he marked the passing of the great Van McCoy by breaking one of his records on air. Nice.

It's safe to say that four-to-the-floor, clicky syncopated guitar and rolling, melodic bassline- infused disco records had been around a while at this point. The term is a shortening of the word 'discotheque' which in the original French meant 'record library'; you could say that disco rises out of Second World War France when Nazi occupiers banned live music, leaving the dance halls with no choice but to play discs. These may well have been the first discos, events where people come together to listen to tracks they could easily hear at home but where the atmosphere, dancing and collective euphoria takes them to another place.

The beginning of the disco explosion as we now know it, however, occurs in 1974 when George McCrae's 'Rock Your Baby', written and produced by Harry Wayne Casey and Richard Finch of KC and the Sunshine Band, becomes the first disco number one on both sides of the Atlantic. The purist will drag you back to 1972 when Cameroonian saxophonist Manu Dibango's 'Soul Makossa' stakes a claim on being the first disco record. However, Isaac Hayes' soul/funk masterpiece 'Theme From Shaft' is actually released at the back end of 1971 and, though its slower tempo may not immediately identify it as disco, it does have that insistent dancefloor groove – so Isaac may have it. And who was going to take that away from him?

Though I never got the chance to meet Isaac Hayes, I get the feeling he was not a man to be messed with. I say this, feeling closer to him having been to the Stax Museum of American Soul Music in Memphis and seen his car. Isaac took delivery of this beast, hand-built to order, in 1972 while presumably congratulating himself on having made the first disco smash by smoking a large cigar in a fur coat, festooned in neck chains and in the company of several ladies on an ivory leather banquette. But 'showing out' had to be possible for someone like Mr Hayes wherever they were and so a car that caught the attention was essential. This baby was a deep green Cadillac with fur-lined interior and gold-plated bumpers, fender and windscreen wipers. And why not? If you're Isaac Hayes in Memphis cruising the Beale Street strip in 1972 there is no good reason not to have gold windscreen wipers.

In late 1978, in the midst of the disco revolution, and back in Chicago, Steve Dahl's radio station WLUP decided to embrace the nascent scene and – a matter of months before the Comiskey Park event cemented his infamy – dispensed with his services accordingly as he was so vociferously opposed to the new sound. Now, most of us when we've been 'let go' will be pretty miffed. We might go to the nearest bar with a few workmates glancing at their wristwatches and shooting terrified 'don't leave me alone with him' looks at each other. We might just go home, pour a gin and tonic and think it might all be for the best. We might drain the whisky bottle from the third drawer down in the desk and punch the boss in the face. It won't be. Steve Dahl does none of these things, though. What Steve Dahl decides to do is to enlist his chums over at Comiskey Park to schedule a match between the White Sox and the Detroit Tigers where there will be a ceremonial burning of disco records at half-time. Yes, you read that right.

The equivalent here in the UK would be that I, a radio DJ and Manchester City fan, decide that it falls on me to rid the world of the curse of Country and Western music. This is hypothetical, you understand, as I have nothing against Country and Western music and in fact visited the Country Music Hall of Fame when I was in Nashville and took a photograph of Hank Williams' suit, noting how much it looked like him even without Hank in it. But wanting to make a stand and turn back the tide of Country I get in touch with my contacts at the Etihad Stadium and ask if during a match against Liverpool, I can collect in large skips the records everyone has brought along as sacrificial offerings to launch a

great conflagration in the middle of the pitch at half-
time. I think I know what Manchester City's response
to this idea would be – but amazingly Steve Dahl's idea
was received enthusiastically at Comiskey Park.

And so it was that on 12 July 1979, Dahl's event went
ahead under the banner 'Disco Demolition Night' and
became a key moment in the Disco Sucks! movement.
This was a campaign launched by white rock fans and
supported by right-wing media and FM rock radio
stations to oppose the emerging sounds. Why would
anyone try to abolish something that so many other
people enjoyed and which didn't hurt anyone? It's not
like Prohibition which, however misguided, could always
claim a higher ground on the basis of health, I suppose.
Dahl was essentially saying it was okay for one group
to have fun and hear their chosen tracks on the radio
but a whole other swathe of people should be denied
that pleasure.

The first game of the evening ended in victory for the
Tigers before the skip of disco records people had
presumably bought to donate – or already had bought
and so secretly quite liked – was dragged to the middle
of the diamond and detonated. At this point some of
the crowd, which had been expected to be around twenty
thousand but actually was nearer to fifty thousand, sent
into a trance by the potency of the ritual, invaded the
pitch and tore up chunks of the hallowed turf. This
meant that the second match couldn't be played and so
was awarded to the Tigers. What a cracking night that
was. Some numbskulls torched some records, the White

Sox lost twice and the pitch was ruined. But what was it about disco that so incensed these people? And is a class and colour – even gender – divide evident in the answer? After all, this was an event described by Dave Marsh of *Rolling Stone* as 'your most paranoid fantasy about where the ethnic cleansing of rock radio could ultimately lead'.

The problem is certainly linked to the Summer of Love revolution which was an almost exclusively white phenomenon. If you look at photographs of Woodstock in 1969, the ultimate gathering of the countercultural clans, you will see an ocean of white faces. And occasionally a good deal more pallid flesh than that thanks to the bearded, sallow souls who have decided that the experience of listening to Country Joe and the Fish is best enjoyed with one's testicles on display. And if you look at the artists who performed across three days you will only find five acts who could be described as being people of colour: Jimi Hendrix, Ravi Shankar, Santana, Sly and the Family Stone and Richie Havens.

Of course the hippie and disco movements were in a sense looking for the same thing: an escape from the drudgery of everyday life and mundane jobs. However, whereas the Woodstock hordes were dropping out and smoking themselves into a somnambulistic haze while the Grateful Dead played for what felt like eight hours, the disco fraternity persevered with the nine-to-five existence throughout the week to be able to afford the best clothes to enhance the best possible Saturday night. The hippies may well have been happy to writhe in front of Michael Shrieve from Santana's drum solo wearing a halter top woven out of seaweed, but if you were clubbing you wore your very best clothes as a badge of honour.

This sartorial pride was nothing new – as the Teddy boys and the Mods in particular had all spent massive amounts of modest disposable income on the very best attire to show out at the weekend. Okay, so you couldn't afford a gold-plated, fur-lined car like Isaac Hayes, but you could afford a very good suit if you forewent the odd burger, egg and chips at a Wimpy Bar. In a sense, this intersection of music and fashion ushers in the cult of the designer label although the modern mode of logo adornment is arguably a more crass expression of wealth. Getting a hand-cut outfit so the money spent is in the tailoring and the cloth is one thing; buying something at an inflated price off-the-peg, just so you can display the manufacturer's branding, is wholly another. Once, while waiting in my barber's for another fine tuning of my meticulous coiffure, I read an interview with someone who I'll refrain from naming, as you won't have heard of him anyway, who was evidently a 'fitness guru'. He was discussing his Rolex watch of which he said: 'It's not a status symbol, it just shows you are successful', i.e. exactly what a status symbol does.

Another major difference between the whitey Woodstock weirdniks and the dapper dancefloor denizens was that the former still worshipped the cult of the superstar rocker – Eric Clapton was proclaimed God at one point – whereas the latter worshipped the sense of community the club scene brought them. This was true of the Northern Soul movement in England which just pre-dated the golden age of disco. Three legendary venues drew crowds, weekend after weekend, who travelled the country just to dance. The Twisted Wheel in Manchester began its all-nighters in the late Sixties, followed by the Golden Torch in Tunstall, Stoke-on-Trent, in 1971, and then Wigan Casino in 1973.

If you've worked all week and want a good night out, you don't want to spend any part of it sitting in a draughty municipal concert hall waiting for The Nice to decide to start playing. You want to get to the venue and throw yourself into a party that's already up and running. The democracy of the dancefloor is something that runs throughout popular musical history and prob-ably hits its high point at the illegal acid house raves of the late Eighties, although intriguingly a lot of those events and the locations and clothing involved owed more to Woodstock than Studio 54. Perhaps in a sense the hippies got something right: the ultimate egalitarian ecstasy-fuelled event meant that nobody cared what you were wearing.

However, it's hard not to be drawn back to thoughts of a racial prejudice here, since disco only really became huge in mainstream terms when it was fronted by three of the whitest whities imaginable: the Bee Gees. The film *Saturday Night Fever* hit the screens in 1977 and the soundtrack remains the eighth best-selling album of all time having shifted over 40 million copies. Unforgettably the film tells the story of Tony Manero, played by John Travolta, who comes from low Brooklyn stock and has a dead-end job in a paint store, but lives for the weekend nightlife and the coterie of friends, and indeed adversaries, that come with it. This is the disco dictum writ large. Yes, your weekday life is grim, but with a white suit and the right moves, you can be a star on a Saturday night. Equally, you can hide on the dancefloor knowing that you are amongst friends – perhaps why the disco scene became so important to the gay community, particularly in New York.

Discos were places where nobody judged, except for Studio 54 where punters were hand-picked by imperious doormen, the lights were low and anything went. Drugs played a part of course – as cannabis and LSD did for the hippies, amphetamine did for the Northern Soul clubgoers and ecstasy did for the ravers. In fact Quaaludes became known as 'disco biscuits'. But for those who felt discriminated against, the discos became a safe haven to the extent that by 1978 Village People were able to celebrate the gay lifestyle on the streets of the Big Apple with one of the greatest party anthems ever recorded: 'Y.M.C.A.'. There is still something utterly joyful about watching cowboy Randy Jones in his chaps gleefully performing those simple moves with his stereotyped bandmates and representing that disco could be for everyone. If disco sucked it was only to draw people in and share the love.

Of course the euphoria of the late Seventies would be

short-lived as the shadow of AIDS invaded the scene with catastrophic and heartbreaking results just a few years later. Given its full name of acquired immune deficiency syndrome it transmitted the HIV virus between people and decimated the gay community in particular. It was seized upon by conservative factions and evangelical preachers as evidence that God's disdain had been cast down on a plague of hedonistic heathens. Yet more grist to the anti-disco mill.

Released the same year as 'Y.M.C.A.', Gloria Gaynor's 'I Will Survive' was originally the B-side to a song called 'Substitute', first recorded by The Righteous Brothers. Ostensibly 'I Will Survive' is a simple lyric about a woman who's been dumped by her bloke, who tells him that she's going to be fine and is better off without him. Yet somehow the song's message became one of not only female empowerment but also gay pride and just the confidence to be yourself. This is central to the disco scene. The show is not about the pampered popinjays on the stage but about everybody in the house. Gloria would later have another massive hit with 'I Am What I Am' in 1983, reinforcing the message. But 'I Will Survive' has become disco's ultimate anthem, and as a measure of how far the genre has come since that night at Comiskey Park in 1979 – when even the esteemed magazine *Time* was moved to call disco music 'a diabolical thump-and-shriek' – this song has now been selected by the National Recording Registry at the Library of Congress as a track of major cultural significance. Nobody's burning it now.

4

I Hear a New World

The early Sixties forced a change of perspective as space travel promised a new age of exploration, discovery and at least the possibility of life beyond our own world. There were, in a sense, crossroads moments for many of us. This was certainly true for a man called Joe Meek who not only took musical inspiration for his groundbreaking work from the space race, but also formulated the revolutionary notion that the recording studio could be an instrument in itself and not just somewhere you went to make music.

On 10 July 1962, a Thor-Delta rocket blasted off from Cape Canaveral carrying a precious payload: Telstar. The artificial earth satellite, Sputnik, was actually launched in October 1957 but as it wasn't immortalised in a pop record recorded in a flat above a leather goods shop on London's Holloway Road, it need not concern us here.

Telstar 1, which was followed not unreasonably by Telstar 2 in May 1963, somehow looked and felt like the future, which may be why it so inspired the maverick Meek to create 'space rock'. In 1951 the Festival of Britain had presented events across the UK, including an exhibition on the South Bank which was advertised with modernist graphics that seemed to point to the future. One of the exhibits was the Skylon which was a three hundred-feet-high steel structure with – and in this sense it was likened to the parlous British economy of the time – no visible means of support. It could loosely be described as 'cigar-shaped', albeit a cigar with very narrow ends, the sucking of which might result in an embolism. Its name is a composite of pylon, sky and nylon, all of which were shortly to revolutionise our lives. For sure nylon stockings had been around for a couple of decades but here we were on the brink of such life-enhancing items as the nylon bed sheet and the drip-dry shirt. Which of us of a certain age can forget the unadulterated thrill of waiting for the discharge of static as you leapt into your nylon-clothed bed to escape the chill of the non-centrally heated house where ice could be a feature not exclusively reserved for the outside of windows, but the inside too. The nylon shirt was another enhancement of modern life. In the mid-Sixties I had two, both of which are indelibly stamped on my memory to this day. One was a lilac polo neck which zipped up the back. No, really. And the other was a white one with a lace ruffle. Mum, thanks for nothing. The drip-dry boast was actually in relation to time saving on wash day and the amount of sweat generated from the often deodorant-free underarm areas made this a feature to be grateful for on a daily basis. The Skylon, though, like the graphics, seemed to fascinate and beguile with its representation of a brave and pioneering future that lay just around the corner from postwar austerity.

Telstar similarly looked like the future: it was quite small, being a rough sphere less than three feet in diameter. But it was silvery and metallic, with all sorts of panels attached. It looked rather like two R2D2s had been decapitated and their heads welded together. When in orbit Telstar beamed back telegraph images, telephone calls and the first transatlantic TV pictures of the Statue of Liberty, the Eiffel Tower and part of a baseball game taking place at Wrigley Field in Chicago between that city's Cubs and the spectacularly unimaginatively named Philadelphia Phillies. Here in the UK we could take pride in the fact that one of only six of the project's terrestrial radio 'ground stations', designed for telecommunications with spacecraft, was at Goonhilly Downs in Cornwall, which had the benefit of excellent nomenclature. There was also a room full of technical gubbins monitored by boffin-ish blokes in white coats with many biros in their top pockets and very few girlfriends at BBC TV Centre in London's Shepherd's Bush.

The unlikely progenitor of space rock, and creator of the worldwide hit inspired by Telstar, was born in Newent, Gloucestershire, in 1929. Evidently a radio and electronics nut, the young Joe Meek filled his parents' garden shed with all manner of electrical gadgets, which he tinkered with endlessly. After a spell working for the Midlands Electricity Board he went on to a production company who supplied programmes to Radio Luxembourg before becoming a fledgling record producer. His first hit was 'Bad Penny Blues' by Humphrey Lyttelton which was released on Parlophone in 1956 but not before Humph and the precocious knob-twiddler had almost come to blows over the mix. Meek's temperament clearly belied his name, as would become increasingly obvious as time went on.

In 1960 he established Triumph Records from his three-storey flat in Islington – a modern-day estate agent might well describe it as a 'triplex' – above a shoe and leather goods shop at 304 Holloway Road. From these humble premises with recording equipment littered throughout the dowdy rooms, Meek and his accomplices, notably Reading-born Geoff Goddard, quickly created a series of otherworldly sounding records. An early Triumph release was the 1960 EP *I Hear a New World*, which contained tracks from a full concept album dubbed by Meek as 'an outer space music fantasy', but which would not see a full release until 1991 as it was deemed to be of such low commercial interest.

And then came the hits. The Goddard-composed 'Johnny Remember Me' was a smash for John Leyton in 1961, followed later by Tornados bass man Heinz Burt with 'Just Like Eddie' in 1963 and the Honeycombs' 'Have I the Right?' in 1964. For the latter the thumping drum sound was partially created by all the members of the band stomping on the wooden stairs, an example of the creative approach to recording that was characteristic of Meek's modus operandi. It was also indicative of a deteriorating relationship between the nascent British Phil Spector and his landlady Violet Shenton. Apparently when the noise from the rented rooms above became too intrusive she would thump on the ceiling with a broom. Ever the peacemaker, the irascible Meek would position speakers in the stairwell to bombard the emporium below with his sonic explorations.

But back then Meek was undiagnosed bipolar and – though undoubtedly a genius – without the treatment he would have received today, was not someone who could be relied upon for sound decision-making. A situation little helped by his copious intake of amphetamines and barbiturates. He advised Brian Epstein not to bother with The Beatles, and refused to sign one group unless they got rid of their lead singer: the sixteen-year-old Rod Stewart.

He visited churchyards where he set up tape recorders to make contact with voices beyond the grave. In this he seems to have been unsuccessful though he did claim that the nocturnal mewings of a cat were messages in a different language if they could only be decoded. In a sense I suppose he was right. The cat was undoubtedly communicating something to the neighbourhood moggy massive and though I'm no expert I imagine the gist of the communiqué was, 'Does anyone fancy a shag? Or failing that, a fight?'

Undeterred, Meek claimed that he was spoken to in his dreams by Buddy Holly and that his flat had become a drop-in centre for poltergeists, although if the evidence for this was knocking sounds coming from the walls and floors it seems more likely to have been Mrs Shenton attacking the cornicing with a broomstick in order to flog a pair of sling-backs to a beehived harridan from Angel in peace. Whatever was, or wasn't, going on was enough to convince Joe that someone was out to get him – quite possibly, in his mind, the Krays. Such was his paranoia that he rarely left the flat without wearing thick sunglasses. It's also worth bearing in mind that he was a homosexual when it was still illegal and so feelings of persecution were unsurprisingly never far away. His mental state deteriorated to such an extent that it brought about his tragic demise when, on 3 February 1967, he killed Violet Shenton with a single barrel shotgun before turning the weapon on himself.

Meek's best-known work remains the track 'Telstar', released in August 1962, which went to number one in both the UK and the American charts. It was in fact only the second *Billboard* Hot 100 chart-topper from a British artist, following the distinctly more earthbound strains of West Country clarinetist Acker Bilk's 'Stranger on the Shore'. The Tornados can therefore stake a claim to being the first band from these islands to be transatlantic hit parade toppers. And they were a band, even if they had been hand-picked by Meek as his house posse of session musicians. In fact, while we're talking about chart performance, we should note that the Tornados' drummer, Clem Cattini, holds the record for having played on the most UK hits of anyone ever and is on at least forty-four UK number ones. His bandmates have slightly less illustrious pedigrees, perhaps, being guitarists Alan Caddy, who was also in Johnny Kidd and the

Pirates, and George Bellamy, whose son Matt is the front man of *Mad Max* pomp-prog pyrotechnical Teignmouth trio Muse. The bass player was the aformentioned Heinz Burt, a blond dreamboat who would later tour as a solo artist backed by the mighty Canvey Island cock robins Dr Feelgood, and who has the unfortunate distinction of being the original owner of the fatal shotgun.

The Tornados had a handful of subsequent hits, one of which was called 'Robot'. If you want to gleefully waste three minutes of your life then look for the video clip for this track on YouTube. In it, the members of the group, wearing silver helmets that are, in equal part, Cyberman and Norman Conquest, frolic in some bedrag-gled looking forest while playing the tune. There are no drums in evidence, however, so I assume Clem Cattini is one of two figures indulging in some strangely under-whelming robotic dancing and canoodling with a pair of unhelmeted earth maidens, who are clearly keen to learn the basis of robot love. Sadly, the party is broken up when our amateurish automatons light a campfire and are promptly seen off by some gendarmes with guard dogs.

No such gripping location footage accompanies 'Telstar', sadly, but what of its haunting tones? To a large degree, the intergalactic sound used to such telling effect is created by one of the very first electronic instruments: the clavioline. This device can perhaps be acknowledged as the first generally available 'synthesizer'. Created in Versailles in 1947, by Constant Martin, the clavioline sold thirty thousand units in Great Britain alone. There are, however, even earlier electronic instruments that might challenge the clavioline. Beloved of Radiohead lead guitarist Jonny Greenwood and French twentieth-century classical composer Olivier Messiaen, the Ondes Martenot was designed and unveiled in 1928, the same year that Soviet Léon Theremin launched his titular device. The Ondes Martenot produced sound by the movement of rings along a wire, in rather the same way that I used to try and fail to win a prize annually when trying to do just that at the church bazaar, where a buzzer attached to an Ever Ready battery would let off a catastrophic buzz as I attempted to round the last corner of the electrified wire game, which appeared impossible to navigate for anyone who wasn't double-jointed.

There are accounts of an electronic instrument having appeared as early as 1748, using the principles of electromagnetism to vibrate strings in much the same way as an EBow works on a guitar. This seems scarcely credible, as electromagnetism was not generally accepted and understood until the 1820s, though that doesn't rule out the possibility that Czech research pioneer and preacher Václav Prokop Diviš may have produced a single model to install in his church somewhere in the mid-1700s. Using the methods it did to reproduce string and brass timbres and tones, it is sometimes referred to as an orchestrion, though why would you call it that when you can use the name he gave it: 'The Golden Dionysus'? Okay, there's a slight whiff of Corfu discotheque to the name, but in 1748? Dare to dream, Vàclav, dare to dream.

However, the generally accepted first synth-type-thing to be made vaguely available was the telharmonium concocted by the Iowan inventor and scholar of the physics of music, Thaddeus Cahill. Based on the operation of tone wheels, and sharing some functions with the Hammond organ, it was readily available around 1897 at an equivalent price today of around five million dollars. No wonder Casio eventually spotted a gap in the market. And even if you could afford a telharmonium, there were other problems associated with it. The entry-level model was said to have weighed around seven tons, while the full all-singing, all-dancing top-of-the-range beast with all the bells and whistles came in at a frankly staggering two hundred tons. Transportation was therefore tricky and involved thirty locomotive boxcars. This would seem to be enough to put off any travelling band. That said, if they'd been around it's tempting to think that Emerson, Lake & Palmer would have given it a go.

But if it's difficult to exactly pinpoint the birth of the devices which made electronic music possible, we can lay the founding stone of space rock at 304 Holloway Road. Inspired by aural possibilities, captivated by the concept of deep space and prone to flights of fancy about what music of other spheres might sound like, Joe Meek not only started space rock in 1960 but had an international smash hit with it only two years later. This is fully five years before Cambridge cosmologists Pink Floyd bring us 'Astronomy Domine' and 'Interstellar Overdrive' on their 1967 debut album, *The Piper at the*

Gates of Dawn. Not until over a decade after 'I Hear a New World' did Hawkwind fire up the old audio generator and set off *In Search of Space* in 1971.

Gradually musical space travel became more and more accessible and eventually ELO and Earth, Wind & Fire routinely arrived on stage in spacecraft while Parliament/Funkadelic's mothership hovered somewhere nearby. And who can forget The Orb's 1991 album, *Adventures Beyond the Ultraworld,* where once they'd blasted through the little fluffy clouds they witnessed a 'Supernova at the End of the Universe'.

It was Joe Meek who started this cosmic exploration before handing on the baton to David Bowie whose 1969 classic 'Space Oddity' and its marooned hero Major Tom focused on a theme later echoed in the 2009 film *Moon* in which Sam Rockwell plays lone astronaut Sam Bell abandoned on a lunar base. The film's director? Duncan Jones, the man who fell to a more earthly name after being christened Zowie by his parents, David and Angie Bowie.

Oh yes, a couple more things about 'Telstar'. The track was the favourite pop song of Margaret Thatcher. Make of that what you will. But the other thing to think about is that though it is of course long inoperative, Telstar 1 is still up there and will pass over your head sometime soon.

5

The Writing on the Wall

There's nothing I can tell you about Kurt Donald Cobain that you don't already know. Except possibly that his middle name was Donald. The Donald, maybe. Not the most promising opening to a chapter but it's true. He was born in Aberdeen, Washington, just ahead of the Summer of Love on 20 February 1967. He had a poor and troubled childhood but like so many other kids sought to form a band to escape his demons, if only it could be successful. His band did indeed become successful, very successful, but Kurt's demons stayed with him. He killed himself in Seattle with a shotgun on 5 April 1994, joining the famous list of rockers who checked out at the age of twenty-seven. So there you have it. The Kurt Cobain story. The end.

Except his music meant his story was far from over. When 'Smells Like Teen Spirit' was released in 1991, it sent a clarion call around the globe. I can still remember vividly lying in bed and hearing it come on Simon Mayo's breakfast show on the now defunct Radio One and thinking, 'What the hell is this?' It had everything. Phenomenal musicianship, raw power and a great tune. It was clear to anyone with ears that something truly remarkable had been created here by three scruffy blokes who looked like they'd come to do a spot of landscape gardening, and that the world had shifted slightly on its axis. To their credit the good people of France, Spain, Belgium and New Zealand recognised this immediately and sent it to the toppermost of the poppermost. Sorry, lapsed into archaic DJ-speak for a moment there. Sent it to number one, I mean. In the UK it reached number seven, and six in the US.

What was it about this pop song that so galvanised the Earth's youth who leapt on board? In a way, it got to the core of what the rock and roll business is about: it managed to sound like the way the kids listening to it felt. Capturing the hearts and minds of the youth market is fiendishly difficult to do. Yes, of course there have been many pop megastars, but how many times has some kind of hysteria seemingly enveloped the whole planet? Certainly, the hip-wiggle of Elvis came close to achieving it, as did The Beatles. Though we might now find it uncomfortable, Michael Jackson had a similarly seismic effect. It's also instructive to look back at the genuine tidal wave of teenage fanaticism that accompanied the Bay City Rollers wherever they went for a time. But how did this plaid-shirted urchin from a two-bit logging town and his towering henchmen make a record whose producer Butch Vig said of it: 'It reminds me a little bit of how Bob Dylan's songs affected people in the sixties. In a way, I feel the song affected a generation of kids in the nineties. They could relate to it.'?

And so we find ourselves at a crossroads once again. A point of intersection, where one man's yelps of frustration hit home with fans waiting for an eruption like this, right across the globe. So how did Kurt and Nirvana make it happen?

Certainly Nirvana were great players and created a hell of a maelstrom of noise for a three-piece. I can confirm this personally as I was on the side of the stage for their now legendary performance as bill-toppers at the Reading Festival in 1992. Never in all my years of festival-going has one event been so dominated and consumed by the prospect of a set by a headline act. It was as if the whole weekend built to that moment, to the extent that it seemed impossible that they could live up to expectations. Except they did. Cobain was, at that time, the biggest rock star in the world and yet so obviously ill-equipped to deal with the fame bestowed upon him. Waiting for his arrival on stage to witness at close hand how he dealt with that pressure started to feel almost voyeuristic. And when he was wheeled out on a trolley in medical robes, it seemed like he was making a reference to his acute struggle. Nirvana were incendiary that day. That three people could make a noise that colossal seemed to contradict the laws of nature. They were the greatest 'power trio' I have ever seen.

And yet, as a rock 'power trio' they slightly veered from the norm: perceived wisdom is that there is no hiding place when there are so few of you in the band, so this puts a lot of pressure on the guitarist, who is ostensibly playing the only lead instrument. This is certainly true of, say, The Jimi Hendrix Experience, ZZ Top or Muse. However, other famous trios had adjusted the blueprint before Nirvana. Yes, Eric Clapton was a brilliant guitar player capable of carrying any band, but in the band Cream he was accompanied by the combustible partnership of bassist Jack Bruce and drummer Ginger Baker who seemed determined to play as many notes as Eric. Similarly, Rush can sound like they all want to be the lead guitarist but that's prog rock for you. Perhaps going one better were Emerson, Lake & Palmer who also all wanted to be the lead guitarist even though they didn't have a guitarist. (Well, Greg Lake strummed an acoustic occasionally, but you know what I'm saying.) In The Police it often seemed that Andy Summers was creating a raft of delicate and intricate notes on which floated Sting's bass and particularly Stewart Copeland's reggae-infused drums. A punkier proposition like The Jam could, by their very nature, not be about guitar heroics and so Bruce Foxton's bass was often to the fore.

In their considerable armoury, Nirvana had one of the greatest rock drummers ever to have lived in Dave Grohl, although the greatest rock and roll drummer who ever lived is generally accepted to have been the late John 'Bonzo' Bonham of Led Zeppelin. Sadly I never got to see him play live as I stupidly turned down a ticket to see Zep at Earl's Court in May 1975, simply because I couldn't be bothered to go all the way to that there London – and anyway, they were bound to play Bolton Town Hall sometime, weren't they? No, they were not, and so I bitterly regret this now.

I take solace, therefore, in having seen perhaps the second-best rocker drummer of all time – Grohl – from the side of the stage at the Reading Festival in 1992. Like Bonham, here in Grohl was the perfect combination of the power of an artillery battery harnessed to impeccable technique. Oh, and a bit of showbiz. Grohl wasn't blond, but he did flick back his dark tresses like the girl in the Timotei advert having an alfresco shampoo and rinse on the telly. And of course, you knew that the drum kit wasn't going to survive the tumultuous finale to the show. Lofty bassist Krist Novoselic had a deeply resonant tone, which oozed musicality, leaving Kurt, The Donald, to take the role of rhythm guitarist. Of the three of them, his guitar often seemed the least lead instrument, although that's understating it to some extent. Towards the end of their short career Nirvana's guitar parts became emphasised at gigs with the addition of second guitarist Pat Smear who remains a member of Dave Grohl's band Foo Fighters to this day.

Amongst their grunge compatriots then, Nirvana were easily the best musicians so was it that that drew the kids towards them? Well, to some extent, perhaps, but, unlike in jazz, rarely have rock and pop fans been drawn to musicianship alone so that can't be the full explanation.

Their breakthrough track's origins lie in Kathleen

Hanna, a friend of Cobain's, scrawling 'Kurt Cobain smells like Teen Spirit' on the wall of an apartment. Teen Spirit is a deodorant popular amongst teenage girls in the States in the same way that Impulse would be here. Kurt didn't routinely douse himself in this fragrant spray, but his girlfriend of the time Tobi Vail did, and as Kurt was keen to routinely douse himself in Tobi Vail, it was probably a fair observation. So the use of such a prosaic cosmetic product in a track performed by three guys who looked like deodorant might be the last thing on their shopping list gave it a connection to the kids who were going through puberty and trying to decide what level of personal grooming suited them.

In a similarly contradictory fashion, the video featured cheerleaders. Cheerleaders of course symbolise sporting excellence and the clean-cut preppy lifestyle, as far from the world of Nirvana as it was possible to imagine. Legend has it that the cheerleaders were recruited from a local strip club but whether or not that's true is irrelevant. The contrast between the pom-pom-toting primped cheerleaders and the road-sweeper chic of the band could not be more pronounced, so what is being said here? Is the message that you don't need to be on the football team or one of the most glamorous pupils in school to succeed? And not only that but if you achieve success on your own terms, sticking it to the teachers who said you'd never amount to anything, will the prettiest girls and the supposed 'cool' kids be drawn to you anyway? Was Kurt reaching out to adolescent misfits everywhere who were struggling to fit in and reassuring them that if a no-mark like him could overachieve through sheer persistence, then it could be possible for them, too? Perhaps he didn't think that deeply about it, but the message of that song and its video is that the cheerleaders are dancing to Nirvana's tune and where is the star college quarterback now? Probably logging in Aberdeen.

Nirvana had a great composition, a great video, could play really well and injected a forcible sentiment. But what exactly seized these elements and took 'Smells Like Teen Spirit' to the next level? What stamped it indelibly on the frontal lobe? Well, there's only one part of the jigsaw left to examine and that is the voice.

Kurt Cobain came seventh in an MTV poll of the greatest singers in pop and rock, which is interesting as there are plenty of people who will contest that he can barely sing at all. I'm not one of them: I think he's distinctive, the right singer for that band and actually perfectly in tune; and in any case most of my favourite singers have quirks that divide people as to whether they are good vocalists or not. The prime suspect here will always be Bob Dylan. Part of Dylan's milieu was that the message was in the lyrics and these could only be fully appreciated if you stripped away the artifice and sheen of showbusiness in pop recording. The message was important – not the messenger. Many of the Dylan songs that were early hits were covered by people like The Byrds who jingle-jangled their way up the charts with utterly brilliant but nevertheless easier-on-the-ear versions of His Bobness's songs. Dylan, to this day, sometimes seems to deliberately mangle some of his own compositions to the point where they are barely recognisable. This, following on from Butch Vig's observation, is another connection to Nirvana, who would often play inept versions of 'Smells Like Teen Spirit' live – including that night at Reading – to demonstrate that being performing show ponies was not their way.

One of The Byrds was of course David Crosby, who went on to form one of the finest ever close-harmony acts in Crosby, Stills and Nash. Oh, and Young. Sometimes. But back in a dingy and dank Toronto rehearsal room when Neil Young got together with his mates to forge a band, when he started to sing, didn't the others look at each other and think, 'Well, clearly this isn't going to work, is it?' To say his voice is not the stuff of traditional lead vocalist is an understatement. But in the same way that Jonathan Donohue of Mercury Rev's gossamer-thin, reedy voice floats like some kind of incandescent dragonfly over their sumptuous soundtracks, so Neil Young's trebly croak sounds poignant and perfect. Tom Waits was always gruff from the minute he opened his account with the *Closing Time* album in 1973, but he has gradually refined – if that's the right word – his vocal style to sound like a tramp expectorating early morning phlegm into a skip. And let me be clear, I say this as an uberfan. My disappointment at missing Led Zeppelin live is matched by a wistfulness at having failed to catch Tom Waits in concert. Of course Tom is still very much alive and so I live in hope.

At the dawn of glam rock when Bowie and T. Rex first turned my head, I was also drawn to the mysterious though catchy art school rock of the ever-so-slightly sleazy Roxy Music, but has Bryan Ferry sung ever so slightly flat for his whole career? If he has, it is a masterstroke, as they have made many classic albums with a lead voice that is totally unique and unmistakable – if sometimes appearing to operate within its own definition of pitch.

Sometimes perfection is not what you're intending to achieve. It is 'feel' or 'swing' or 'groove' – one of those intangible and inexplicable qualities that transform a good record into a great one. There are no great bands who do not have a great drummer but there are drummers who play slightly behind the beat like Charlie Watts of the Rolling Stones and Simon Kirke of Free and Bad Company. This might sound counterintuitive, as how can the person supplying the beat play behind it? Again, it is a matter of 'feel and 'swing' and 'groove' and gives those tracks their particular swagger.

John Lydon could never be described as a 'singer' in the conventional sense and yet his voice, and glare, are the lasting testimony to the days when punk rockers stalked the earth. Do Lou Reed's curmudgeonly growlings, both solo and in The Velvet Underground, constitute 'real singing'? And yet it is often said that though none of the VU's original albums made the American Top 100, everyone who saw them was inspired to form a band. Is Patti Smith a great singer? Is Ian Dury or Morrissey or Siouxsie Sioux? Clearly, yes, they are. Not in the conventional sense, maybe, but you can get any number of people to sing in tune à la cruise-ship cabaret artistes on BBC1 or ITV any Saturday night and clearly none of the singers we've discussed here would get past the audition stage of those TV sweep-net talent shows. So again, we're back to the voice of the outsider, the misfit, being heard and identified with by fans internationally.

And Kurt is a member of this club. Singers who communicate sheer passion and belief when they open their mouths. And he'd been the first person to join the club for a very long time. He'd also managed to channel all the angst and resentments of his upbringing into this one perfect and profound mission statement, 'Smells Like Teen Spirit'. It was his crossroads moment in two senses. It was the point at which everything he had been striving for fell into place perfectly and would also propel him to the superstardom he had always thought would bring him satisfaction. His aggressive delivery on 'Teen Spirit' sets him apart from most performers. Distortion used to be something engineers sought to avoid at all costs, and yet the distorted guitar has formed the backbone of many a rock and roll band. Similarly, pushing a voice to breaking point has been a feature of literally thousands of classic records. The origins of singing this way can probably be traced right back to Robert Johnson's old mate Howlin' Wolf, whose primal scream from his sturdy frame spoke for the impoverished sharecropping men and women forced to work long hours in hundred-degree temperatures for a pittance in the cottonfields of the Mississippi Delta. They felt how he sounded.

Some of the appeal of early rock and roll for the

restless teenagers in search of their own voice could be found in the impassioned howls of Little Richard, from which you can draw a direct line on to James Brown, Michael Jackson and Prince. Some artists made their shrieking a major part of the act, like Screaming Lord Sutch and Screamin' Jay Hawkins. Led Zep's Robert Plant shrieked his way to become the biggest rock star in the world and has been the benchmark for heavy rock singers ever since. Axl Rose has a piercing shrillness to his wailing, which I've never particularly enjoyed myself, but he piloted Guns N' Roses to becoming the biggest band on the planet for a time. Then there's the misfit, feral-looking Eric Burdon of The Animals, who incidentally, on his 2013 solo album *'Til Your River Runs Dry*, recorded a song called '27 Forever', and who positively snarled through the British beat revolution.

Like those artists before him, Cobain sings in a way that exudes pain, angst, passion, resolve, (teen) spirit but also scant regard for his own health. This, again, speaks directly to the young and is part of that nihilistic '27 Club' mentality of 'live fast, die young' that seems so intoxicating when life is stretching out before you indefinitely. If you watch videos of Nirvana live, you will witness the demolition of a lot of equipment, but there are also images of Kurt flinging himself into the drum kit without shielding himself from the impact. He seems to have no thought for his own safety and it's all part of the appeal. Of not conforming. Of not playing safe. Of not looking after yourself. Of being free enough to do whatever you want. All of those emotions and ideas are there in every word sung in 'Smells Like Teen Spirit' and that's what you need if you're going to be the voice of a generation and set the music business off down a different track.

6

An Original Soundtrack

When people listen to the sheer sonic sumptuousness of 10cc's 'I'm Not in Love', it's often with a certain incredulity that it was recorded in the mid-Seventies when the available technology – even in state-of-the-art recording studios – was a tenth of what you've now got in your mobile phone. A figure which, I confess, is a guess on my part.

We do tend to measure tech capacity by comparing whatever object is under consideration to the smartphone permanently attached to our palms these days. Isn't the received wisdom that there was less compu-power in the lunar module that took Neil Armstrong and Buzz Aldrin down to the Sea of Tranquility than there is in your phone on which you've just ordered slippers from Amazon? I'm not quite sure what that tells you, other than that delivery times for online shopping are very quick and that's why Amazon founder Jeff Bezos is the richest man in the world, and yet conversely we still haven't been back to the moon. Come on, you guys at NASA. What have you been doing all this time?

My plan for lunar colonisation, therefore, would seem to be so beautifully simple that the mission control boffins with their comb-over hairstyles and brown pullovers will kick themselves when they read this: we simply order a moon base from Amazon on next-day delivery. 'Yes, Mark, you are clearly some kind of genius', I hear you thinking, 'but how does that constitute "colonisation"? Where are the people?' I'm ahead of you here, and this is perhaps the *really* clever bit. The driver of the van, or commander of the space delivery saucer or whatever, is told to make the moon pods the last drop on the round and then just stay there. That way, you've still got your slippers, but we have satellite settler number one. And then when he or she starts ordering things they're going to need up there, like space suits, food in tablet form, thermal underwear and yes, slippers, the next pilot stays too. I know. It's so obvious there must be a flaw here, but I've been through it up to twice and I can't find it, and, as we've already agreed that I'm a genius, it must be sound.

Anyhow, back to the topic loosely and literally 'in hand'. The mobile phone has almost become a unit of measurement. It's strange how many oddities persist in the area of quantification. Countries or regions are often said to be 'roughly the size of Wales'. Which, if you don't know, is about 8,023 square miles or 20,779 square kilometres. In the interests of comparison and showing how deep a level of research is at work here, I've used the old πr^2 formula to calculate the area of the old Mare Tranquillitatis and come up with a figure of 6,375 square kilometres. Which means, reaching for the calculator on my lunar module trumping phone, that you can fit three into Wales. I hope that will be of some use to you.

But the old school imperial ways of measuring things are generally accepted as: inch, cigarette packet, foot, yard, double-decker bus, football pitch, mile, Wales. Certainly that's what I was taught at school, and was laid out on the back of my Silvine exercise book, and it's served me well as the paragraph above has demonstrated. Even in this metric age, some of these measurements persist. In today's paper I was reading about the world's biggest aircraft, a sort of plane and airship hybrid, the Airlander. It is ninety-three metres in length, but just in case you were having trouble envisaging that, they've illustrated it alongside a Routemaster bus, which measures eleven metres. So that means this behemoth of the skies is as long as eight-and-a-half double-decker buses. Or if you're having trouble envisaging a half-bus then think of eight of them with a long wheelbase Ford Transit bringing up the rear. So this thing is as long as a football pitch is wide.

Anyway, all of the above is to say that, just because things were created in the past, when technology was basic or non-existent, we shouldn't be surprised that they still look or sound great. A painting by J.M.W. Turner or Marc Chagall is in no way reduced in greatness because it comes from an age before the Apple Mac. A masterpiece will always be a masterpiece and a masterpiece is what 'I'm Not in Love' most certainly is.

10cc are kind of a supergroup, by which I mean a coming together of huge talents rather than a conglomeration of household names. Having said that, two of the members had had relatively successful pop careers prior to the formation of the band. Eric Stewart was a member of Wayne Fontana and the Mindbenders though he only became lead singer after Wayne went solo. The Mindbenders sound like they ought to be a leftfield psychedelic outfit but they were in fact purveyors of lightweight melodic beat pop, notably with 'A Groovy Kind of Love' in 1966, preceded by the memorably titled 'Um Um Um Um Um Um' in 1964. Like the other 7.5cc he was from the northwest of England and a Lancashire town called Droylsden.*

Another 2.5cc came in the form of Graham Gouldman. Gouldman had been a member of a reasonably successful beat group called The Mockingbirds though had already discovered a nascent talent for songwriting, composing hits like 'For Your Love' and 'Heart Full of Soul' for the Yardbirds, 'Bus Stop' and 'Look Through Any Window' for The Hollies and 'No Milk Today' for Herman's Hermits. He had a writing contract with a music publishing company in New York, but also maintained

---

* Which was also home to the lead singer of Herman's Hermits, Peter Noone, once memorably paged at an airport as Peter No-One, and Howard Donald of Boyz II Men band Take That.

a presence as a musician in various bands including a stint as stand-in bass player for the Mindbenders.

The other 5cc came as a bit of a less decorous Buckingham/Nicks package deal. Raised in Stockport, Kevin Godley, who had drummed for The Mockingbirds, and Lol Creme had had a couple of stabs at the big time in their duo which was called Frabjoy for some reason, and when that didn't work they renamed themselves Runcible Spoon. Yes, well, perhaps there was an elaborate owl and pussycat conceit here. Perhaps one of them was wise and stayed up all night while the other slept a lot and went to the toilet in a litter tray but who knows? Certainly they were both terrible names for a duo and it's notable that when Kev and Lol left 10cc and became a duo again, they wisely traded as Godley and Creme.

So it's fair to say there was a formidable amount of songwriting, instrumental, vocal and production talent in that small pool of individuals who made up 10cc – named, incidentally, after the standard deposit of the male ejaculation. Either that or a conspicuously under-powered moped. But with so much ability and such strong personalities perhaps it was inevitable that the band would fracture into two double acts after releasing only four albums: the eponymous debut in 1973 and then *Sheet Music* the following year, *The Original Soundtrack* a year after that and *How Dare You!* in 1976. The departure of Godley and Creme came much too soon, and it's tempting to think that a year off might have cleared the air and resulted in many more years of creative outpourings. In some ways they are the UK's answer to Steely Dan in that they are less pop stars than architects of literate, intelligent music that still has a good tune, and they are possibly afforded less respect than is their due.

The same could not be said about their band that immediately preceded 10cc, called Hotlegs, evidently because the hot-panted receptionist at the studios . . . well, you get the idea. Those legs were attached to the torso of one Kathy Redfern and would later enable her to perambulate the short distance from the lobby into the vocal booth where she reluctantly performed the spoken part about big boys not crying in the haunting middle of 10cc's immortal moment.

The recording facility where Kathy Redfern was the first person to greet you as you entered was Strawberry Studios in Stockport, named by engineer Eric Stewart after 'Strawberry Fields Forever'. Now used as humdrum office space, it once witnessed recording sessions by the likes of Neil Sedaka, The Stone Roses and Paul McCartney, who was evidently not put off by the place being named after a Lennon song. Perhaps most legend-arily of all, Joy Division made the classic *Unknown Pleasures* album there. I worked there many times myself, though I can't say I was making recording history in the same way. Though all too aware of the seminal moments that had been captured on tape in those rooms, I was charged as a young producer for the BBC with getting bored session musicians to record an endless chain of bland instrumentals. You may well ask why. In the mid-Eighties the Beeb had an agreement on the amount of 'needle-time' – in other words the number of records they could play. Accordingly various combinations of musicians who could read scores were despatched to Strawberry to knock off copious cover versions of easy-listening tunes to fill the otherwise empty airwaves. It was a fairly dispiriting endeavour. I often used to say I was recording music by musicians who didn't want to play it, to send to radio programmes that didn't want to broadcast it, to audiences who didn't care whether they heard it or not. The only sense of urgency was injected into proceedings by seeing how quickly we could get it done before falling into the welcoming arms of the Waterloo public house just over the road. Still, it was better than working for a living.

Hotlegs was short-lived and seems to have been a studio-based experimental prank to some extent, and so nobody could have been more surprised than they were when their track 'Neanderthal Man' became a number two hit in the UK in 1970. The 'song', if you can really call it that, consists of a chant in which the titular troglodyte invites his female counterpart to enjoy carnal relations accompanied by a primitive drum beat, rudimentary acoustic guitar and recorder. In the video there are the predictable hot-legged women in faux animal-skin bikinis, though Godley, Creme and Stewart seem distinctly uninterested in making the advances that their chant suggests. Classic passive-aggressive behaviour if you ask me. Gouldman was unavoidably detained in New York by his songwriting contract and so doesn't appear in the clip, and though he was probably miffed at the time he's

probably been grateful ever since. Perhaps the cc cave-
men's embarrassment is understandable, but the record
did at least propel them into the charts and make their
collective a genuine hit-making proposition. Incidentally,
if you're wondering what kept them off the top spot it
was Elvis's 'The Wonder of You' and so I think we can
safely say that justice was done and common sense
prevailed.

'I'm Not in Love' appears on *The Original Soundtrack*
album but was by no means a certainty for inclusion in
its early form. Unimaginably, it had started out with a
bossa nova beat, and despite the hours spent on it was
– in the opinion of Kevin Godley at least – 'crap'. In
fact, it was so low down the pecking order of songs
that, due to tape being expensive and reused wherever
possible, no recordings of this early version exist as they
were all erased. Clearly though, the Eureka moment here
was deciding to slow it down and make the vocals very
much the centre of the track. In fact the instrumental
backings are minimal. Yes, the soothing vamp of the
Fender Rhodes piano is key, but the other bits of guitar,
bass, piano and Moog are, while important details, details
nonetheless. Lead vocals are by Eric Stewart, but the
breathy banks of backing vocals are what transforms
the track into a classic and brings them to a crossroads
in the history of recorded music.

So how did they do it? By multitracking of course,
but there was more to it than that. Apart from recording
sound to tape in the first place, multitracking is the single
most important innovation in recording there has ever

been. It's a simple idea. You record something, and then play the tape back, recording something else on top of it without erasing the first thing you laid down, meaning that you gradually build up a textured patchwork of sound. Nowadays you can buy a simple loop pedal that will perform this function, as Ed Sheeran and KT Tunstall have shown, but it's almost impossible to overestimate what a game changer this was. Everything The Beatles recorded prior to 'I Wanna Hold Your Hand' was recorded live to two-track stereo tape. Eventually, utterly beguiled and fascinated by the limitless possibilities an eight-track recording facility gave them, the Fab Four retired from live performance and retreated to the studio, where they got cracking on what *Rolling Stone* magazine voted the greatest album of all-time: *Sgt. Pepper's Lonely Hearts Club Band*.

Remarkably, multitrack recording began in 1922 and this has to be seen as a majorly significant moment in recording as its effect has been utterly transformative. An employee of General Electric called Charles A. Hoxie devised a way of dubbing up to twelve separate instruments onto 35mm film with his marvellously named device the 'pallophotophone' (which literally means 'shaking light sound'). However, things really started to advance with the introduction of stereo in 1943. After that, there was some enthusiasm for three-track recording as this gave you two tracks for the band leaving a whole pristine track for the vocals.

The four-track machine would come to be the industry standard, but it's worth remembering that the first eight-track recorders were produced by tape manufacturer Ampex in the Fifties. The first of these was installed in the home of a man who had already been recognised as such an innovator that one of the classic electric guitars was named after him. Yes, I'm talking about Cyril Stratocaster. I'm not really. Les Paul was not only a brilliant guitarist but a master luthier* and studio pioneer. He started out with a tape machine paid for by Bing Crosby but when, in 1957, he took delivery of the eight-track, the sonic landscape changed for good. The machine didn't come cheap. It cost ninety thousand dollars when a man's average yearly wage was around ten thousand, which explains why it remained out of reach for more or less everybody who hadn't had the success of Les Paul.

However, the four-track brought about a revolution. The Beatles worked on that format at Abbey Road. Brian Wilson, now fully ensconced in the studio while his brothers and the rest of The Beach Boys were away on tour, created his pocket symphonies on four-track before switching to eight-track to do the vocals when Les Garçons de la Plage got back. To do this, he utilised a technique known as 'bouncing down', where his four tracks of instrumental music were mixed to a solitary track. This would then be transferred to eight-track tape which left seven free channels. Of these, six were devoted to the singing of Mike Love, Bruce Johnston, Al Jardine and Brian and his two brothers, Carl and Dennis, with the final track left over for 'sweeteners'.

---

* Someone who makes and/or repairs string instruments.

Eventually inventions like the Tascam Portastudio, a cassette recorder with overdubbing facilities – on one of which Bruce Springsteen recorded his shadowy *Nebraska* album in 1982, brought basic multitracking to within everyone's reach though clearly not to the level of the by now standard twenty-four track machines found in all the top studios. This meant that the possibilities of what you could record were almost limitless and the two records that took it beyond the previously accepted limit were both released, remarkably, in 1975.

After Elton John's 'Candle in the Wind' tribute to Princess Diana and Band Aid's 'Do They Know It's Christmas?', 'Bohemian Rhapsody' is the third best-selling single in UK history. It is quite rightly regarded as a brilliantly enigmatic composition by Freddie Mercury, but also as a towering achievement in recording. The 'operatic' section was said to have taken three weeks to record and there are tales of up to one hundred and eighty overdubs.

All pretty impressive, but if we're being competitive here then 10cc, hunkered down in Strawberry Studios in Stockport, are the winners. To begin with, they were first. *The Original Soundtrack* came out in March 1975 with the single following in May. 'Bo-Rap', as I believe it's acceptable to call it, was released in October with its parent album *A Night at the Opera* hitting the shops the following month. But in addition to that, 10cc's record had even more overdubs than Queen's and here's how it was achieved.

Once they had the idea of making a widescreen sheen

of voices, they needed to multitrack a lot of vocals. This was achieved by lead vocalist Eric Stewart donning the engineer's hat to record Godley, Creme and Gouldman separately singing 'aaaah' for each of the twelve notes of the chromatic scale. So, initially there would have been twelve notes sung individually by three people, giving thirty-six tracks. However, they didn't do each note once each. They did it sixteen times each. You do the maths. No, it's okay, I'll do it: you're just relaxing, reading a book. That gives you twelve notes sung sixteen times by three people giving a grand total of five hundred and seventy-six voices that are on that track. Of course, this all involved some serious bouncing down – a process not without its problems. Not only do you use and reuse the tape almost to breaking point, but some audio hiss is added each time you make a transfer. 'I'm Not in Love' has got hiss all over it, but rather than detracting from the finished mix, it gives it an even more ethereal gloss.

The next problem they had was that a human's ability to sing 'aaaah' is finite: they will run out of breath. This issue was addressed by the use of twelve-foot-long loops of tape, which passed through the playback heads of the tape machine before travelling past a spindle placed several feet away. This meant that the 'aaaah's were now continuous. By routing each of these loops to the main studio desk, each channel could then play a different note, effectively giving you a huge keyboard. The members of the band were then allocated several faders each so they could introduce the notes required to construct the chords. It is a mind-bending achievement that, to my knowledge, no one has attempted since. If they did, they'd probably do it on their mobile phone. Wouldn't be as good, would it though?

7

Talking Real Fast

That rap has become one of the defining genres of our times is not in doubt. From hedonistic party music to the deeply politically committed, with a few regrettable misogynistic detours along the way, it has become a means of expressing the full range of emotions and sentiments. It stands to reason then that the first rap record released with mass crossover appeal, 'Rapper's Delight' from 1979, marks a crucial juncture in the story of pop. Having said that, the guys in The Sugarhill Gang were, in some ways, merely the latest exponents of a centuries-old phenomenon. They may have reached a crossroads but a lot of people had helped to forge the road that took them there.

The oral tradition goes as far back as when man was an inquisitive and adaptable fish, with gills for legs, who crawled out of the primordial soup. Well, to be fair, it's unlikely those first beachcombers had much in the way of language, although we will never really be sure. Sperm whales in groups not only sing songs that travel thousands of miles across the oceans but, get this, they all sing the same song, so some sort of teaching and learning process is going on.*

In the definitive study of the linguistic capabilities of the Neanderthal people by anthropological think-tank Hotlegs, we know that repetition of simple phrases formed the basis of their communication although they had to fall back on quite a lot of grunting when their vocabulary failed them. A bit like when two people have a professional wrestling bout.

Certainly singing and storytelling in public has formed a crucial part of the distillation and preservation of the arts down the ages, especially from the days before print and widespread literacy. Classics from ancient Greece like Homer's *Odyssey* would have been routinely read aloud in public forums. And it would have been quite a long show. The work contains twelve thousand one hundred lines of dactylic hexameter.

The average person reads around three hundred words a minute, which means that if it has taken you more than a minute to reach this point of this chapter you are a bit of a slowcoach, as the word 'slowcoach' was only word two hundred and eighty-one and we're only reaching the three hundredth word just then on 'hundredth'. Also, a reading in front of an audience would

---

* And it is said that one particular type of dinosaur had a very advanced understanding of language and its name was the thesaurus. Ah, jokes.

have been slower to make sure everyone could hear, and therefore longer. There is a talking book of the *Odyssey* which runs for over eleven hours, so if that's an indication of duration I hope there were plenty of intermissions with plentiful ice cream, popcorn and an efficient interval drinks system. It would last as long as the Grateful Dead supporting Ken Dodd and what a night that was.

Rather like the sperm whales, many cultures have passed down strict rules on melody and construct, including the specification of a set number of syllables. The Japanese have their haiku, of course, which is seventeen syllables – no more, no less – although there is a modern move to make the form even more restrictive by reducing it to twelve. I prefer the ancient way rather than five less. That last sentence, underwhelming though it is, is in fact a haiku in that modern idiom. Of course minimising and restricting the form of expression in this way is a highly skilled art, as the noted oral traditionalist John Cooper Clarke demonstrated in the following old-school example (and I may well be paraphrasing here in order to avoid paying Clarkey any royalties as he is always on the road and must be minted by now):

Expressing oneself in seventeen syllables is very diffic.*

---

* Hindu and Buddhist cultures also place great emphasis on a set pattern of syllables in chandas, and special schools called 'gurukuls' that passed all these traditions down to new generations were not uncommon in India.

We're all familiar with the notion of the wandering minstrel, whom we tend to associate with medieval times although there is evidence that performance poets were in evidence in Anglo-Saxon England before the Norman Conquest. To some extent minstrels found favour, board and lodging at court or in the homes of wealthy families until, succeeded by the troubadours, they were forced into their itinerant lifestyle. In some ways they were the first touring musicians though whether they had tabards with their tour dates printed on the back is unknown.

The dissemination of local news by town criers also forms part of the overall picture, but the preservation and awareness of songs and stories rarely written down owes a great deal to the 'song collectors'. This is what was christened by the American folklorist and musicologist Charles Seeger, father of singers Pete, Peggy and Mike, as 'the folk process'. It involves individuals taking it upon themselves to travel widely in search of the songs that define the indigenous culture in any given area, giving the working man and woman their voice.

The noted and cherished folk singer Shirley Collins is not alone in opining that folk music ends when recording begins. I don't agree with her, but I know what she means. The repertoire was at its purest when it was being sung by people on the slave ships, working in the cottonfields, tending the farmland or toiling in the factories. It was at its most pure when being performed in situ by the people who lived the tough lives the songs documented. Once a song was recorded and released on a record with proper distribution and promotion it had, it was felt, become tainted somehow.

Shirley did in fact accompany the celebrated American song collector Alan Lomax on what became known as the 'Southern Journey' across the Deep South of the US between July and November 1959, following a period when the two had become romantically involved. Lomax, a musician himself, had become reasonably well known during an extended stay in the UK, not least because he had fronted a BBC TV series in 1953 called *The Song Hunter*, with the help of a bright young producer called David Attenborough. However, prior to that, Lomax had travelled widely in the States, particularly Michigan and Wisconsin, recording and filming stories and songs, which were placed for posterity in the Library of Congress, where he curated the Archive of American Folk Song between 1937 and 1942.

In England a similar crusade was undertaken by Cecil Sharp. He was born in Camberwell in 1859 and undertook journeys through the shires, often on his bicycle, looking for the authentic folk songs of these islands. Another musician, and for a time the principal of the Hampstead Conservatoire, Sharp also travelled in Australia and the United States, visiting Virginia, North Carolina, Kentucky and Tennessee between 1916 and 1918. But it was his British research that established his reputation. He published a book on his findings called *English Folk Song: Some Conclusions*, and established the English Folk Dance Society in 1911. A keen

observer of Morris dancing, he was also a vocal advocate for the dying arts of sword dancing in the forms
of the long sword in Yorkshire and the rappers in
Northumberland and on Tyneside. The latter is dancing
performed originally by miners utilising flexible steel
blades which are made to lock in intricate ways. In
fact, there are many places in the northeast of England
where you will find use of the word 'rappers' takes you
in that direction rather than towards The Sugarhill
Gang. I spent a wonderful evening in the Cumberland
Arms in Newcastle in a room that served as the local
rappers' clubhouse in the company of Eliza Carthy and
Kate Tempest, who know plenty of the oral tradition
themselves.

Undoubtedly Sharp is one of the crucial voices in
the folk revival, but not everyone supported his work.
There were those who, rather like Shirley Collins, felt
that folk songs and tales somehow died when they
had been taken from the proletariat and passed into
the custody of the bourgeoisie. And in a striking simi-
larity with the other kind of rappers on the mean
streets of the Bronx, performers of that material were
reluctant to be recorded as that was deemed to dilute
the authenticity.

In the Fifties and Sixties, the most notable exponents
of the oral tradition were the beat poets who really
launched the concept of poetry as a performance art
form in the mainstream. The culmination of this was
the International Poetry Incarnation which took place
at the Royal Albert Hall on 11 June 1965. Loosely

'hosted' by Allen Ginsberg, audience members were given flowers as they entered the building and listened to a stream of poets reciting material on various themes, not least opposition to the Vietnam War. Those who were there reported that the auditorium was rich with the smell of marijuana, with myriad paper planes flying through the air. Pictures from that night show Ginsberg at the microphone on a stage littered with blooms and members of the audience lying prostrate, presumably stoned out of their minds. Sounds like a good night out: I've always been less than adept at making paper planes, but I'm an avid poetry fan and very good at lying down and falling asleep at the first whiff of dope fumes.

Ginsberg was the leading light of an American poetry 'rat pack' that also included such names as Jack Kerouac and Gregory Corso amongst others. In the UK, the English poetry revival was also underway, with a generation of wordsmiths who took inspiration not only from poetry of the past but also of the present as put into song by Bob Dylan and The Beatles. With this in mind, it's perhaps not surprising that, although the movement was a national phenomenon, there was a particularly vibrant pocket in Liverpool where poetry and musical happenings took place at the Everyman Theatre. Out of this emerged distinctive voices like Roger McGough, Adrian Henri, Brian Patten and Adrian Mitchell, who would publish books and make records individually, and collectively as the Liverpool Scene.

Since then many diverse voices have followed the trail forged by those pioneers. Linton Kwesi Johnson, Lemn Sissay, Craig Charles, John Hegley, Ian McMillan and Murray Lachlan Young are just a few who have taken poetry to the stage, and we should also acknowledge the person who has been Britain's most popular performance poet for several decades now. She might not fit into our pantheon of beat greats but you can't deny that Pam Ayres has been hugely successful and become much loved, armed with nothing more than words. And here's the thing. To be a poet you don't need anything other than your thoughts, a way with words and a voice. Unlike Dylan, you don't even need a guitar. As Shirley Collins might agree, it is the purest form of expression and, often, protest. Certainly it's not hard to see how the spiky voices of John Cooper Clarke, Seething Wells, Joolz and Attilla the Stockbroker emerged amidst the anger of punk.

And therefore rapping, without swords, became the inevitable next step on the oral tradition's timeline. Like their street corner doo-wop brethren before them, the street kids began to articulate their fears, hopes and issues, but the question was, would anybody 'sell out' and commit it to vinyl?

The key figure at the next stage of the story is Sylvia Robinson. A native New Yorker, she had a moderately successful singing career of her own from the early Fifties, being initially signed to Columbia as Little Sylvia, and was a session backing vocalist for all manner of people including Ike and Tina Turner. Being one smart cookie with an ear to what was happening on the street she founded Sugar Hill Records and became a producer, label boss and Svengali in a world that would become noted for its macho posturing and highly questionable attitudes towards women. You could say there's a crossroads moment here for the role of women in the music business. It was Robinson who hired bassist Chip Shearin and a drummer for seventy dollars to play the riff that underpins 'Rapper's Delight' for fifteen minutes straight. That riff, essentially the central thrust of 'Good Times' by Chic (released earlier that year, 1979), would later be heard by a surprised Nile Rodgers from Chic, at Club Leviticus in New York, leading to a legal action which resulted in Rodgers and his musical partner Bernard Edwards being credited as co-writers of 'Rapper's Delight'. Rightly protective of copyright infringement, Rodgers was nevertheless familiar with the culture from which this new track came, having been taken to street dance and boom-box events by Debbie Harry and Chris Stein of Blondie. In point of fact, you could make a case for Blondie's 'Rapture' being one of the first rap records, coming as it did in late 1980, later than Kurtis Blow's 'The Breaks' but still nearly two years ahead of another Sylvia Robinson project: 'The Message' by Grandmaster Flash & The Furious Five. No doubt Shirley Collins would question the authenticity of Debbie Harry as a voice of the streets, and she might also even point us in the direction of the Last Poets: a seminal African American group of wordsmiths who gave voice to the civil rights struggle over rhythmic backing. She would also encourage us to consider the roots of the genre forged by the much celebrated jazz poet Gil Scott-Heron. These founding fathers laid some of the ground rules for what was to come later, but there were others, like Harry and Stein, who helped to bring it to the attention of the wider musical community. Certainly Chris and Debbie were supporters of the scene and had the Sugarhill guys freestyle on stage with them at their gig at the New York Palladium. So undoubtedly Blondie were quick to latch on to what was happening on the streets of the Big Apple – but not as quick as Sylvia Robinson. So it was that Robinson's label released the first rap record in 1979, and when questioned by Chip Shearin, who was asking what they were recording the riff for, Sylvia replied (in a lean encapsulation of the oeuvre): 'I've got these kids who are going to talk real fast over it.'

So who were these kids?

Michael Wright, aka Wonder Mike, was from New Jersey – as was his bandmate Master Gee or Guy O'Brien as he's known to his mother who is not the mother of hip hop but is nevertheless the mother of a hip hop trailblazer. O'Brien has had an interesting career; being an executive of an air freshener company at one point – and why not? As anyone who has spent time with bands confined to vans or small dressing rooms, air fresheners are not to be sniffed at. Except that they are.

The third member of the crew sadly passed away in

2014. Henry Lee Jackson was actually born in the Bronx and became famous as Big Bank Hank. He was also known for a time as Imp the Dimp, which sounds like an early character from the *Dandy* comic. Again, showing a willingness to work as well as to perform, he was so successful at running the Crispy Crust pizza joint in New York that the owners put him in charge of their new branch over in Eagleton, New Jersey. Here he managed the Cold Crush Brothers and forged his crucial friendships with the rest of the Sugarhill crew and also came to the attention of Sylvia Robinson, a resident of the town.

Perhaps you'd expect such a classic and landmark release to have been an American smash hit. It actually only reached number thirty-six on the *Billboard* Hot 100 though it would be hard to find thirty-five hotter tracks.* 'Rapper's Delight' was, for most people, breaking new ground and so perhaps number thirty-six was perfectly respectable, though interestingly it did go to number one in Canada and three in Britain. Again, in an expression of the DJ culture that was crucial to its gestation, it was the first Top Forty record to be issued exclusively on twelve-inch vinyl in America. Perhaps its release as a seven-inch in Europe prevented it from

---

* In a similar way it is amazing that David Bowie's '"Heroes"' only reached number twenty-four in the UK charts. I mean how can that be? I suppose that sales of the Bowie single were relatively 'low', pun vaguely intended, as most of his fans would buy the album, but still.

becoming the biggest selling twelve-inch of all-time, an honour which is still held by New Order's 'Blue Monday' – despite that group's successful attempt to drive it down the charts by insisting on performing on *Top of the Pops* live and then being a bit rubbish.

Of course, elements of 'Rapper's Delight' have been borrowed or sampled and have turned up in various unlikely places. Spanish girl group Las Ketchup utilised it in a song called 'Bloody Mary', which in the 2006 Athens-held Eurovision Song Contest came twenty-first out of twenty-four entries.* Nevertheless the saucy Spanish songstrels could feel smug with the knowledge that as a massive hit across Europe 'Un Bloody Mary' sold seven million copies more than 'Rapper's Delight'.

How Sylvia Robinson, Wonder Mike and Master Gee feel about this is hard to say though they can hardly claim to be offended by appropriation as they not only nicked the riff from Chic but also 'borrowed' some verses from heavyweight New York rapper Grandmaster Caz who was also known rather marvellously as Casanova Fly. And they can take great heart from knowing that, as a moment of massive cultural significance, the groundbreaking record they made was not only preserved in the National Recording Registry at the Library of Congress in 2011 (where Alan Lomax tended his folk collection all those years ago), but was also immortalised

---

* If you're interested, the bottom three were France, Malta and Israel, and the event was won by prosthetic Tolkienesque Finnish orc rockers Lordi with 'Hard Rock Hallelujah'.

for ever when it was performed on *The Muppets* TV show in 2015 by the Swedish Chef. There can be few higher accolades than that.

8

Against Your Better Judgement

A single note goes 'clung'. A four-second whining sound follows. So what? So plenty – and here's why.

For a band like The Beatles to release a record with distortion and feedback on it was nothing short of revolutionary. To remind ourselves of just how big they were in 1964, look at the footage of them arriving at JFK Airport and check out the *Billboard* Hot 100 from that April, when they occupied the top five places in the chart with 'Can't Buy Me Love', 'Twist and Shout', 'She Loves You', 'I Wanna Hold Your Hand' and 'Please Please Me'. By December of that year, 'I Feel Fine' gave them another in a long line of number ones in the UK hit parade, knocking the Rolling Stones' 'Little Red Rooster' off the top. An amazing achievement for a wildly experimental record. Okay, it's exaggerating to describe 'I Feel Fine' like that, but you have to remember how things were back then. The charts were full of classic records like

The Supremes' 'Baby Love' and 'All Day and All of the Night' by The Kinks. But many of the most successful contemporaries of the Fabs were, and I mean no disrespect here, middle of the road. Val Doonican was at number five with 'Walk Tall' and Petula Clark, Cliff Richard, Matt Monro and The Bachelors were all there or thereabouts. Major artists all, but hardly the voices of teenage angst and revolution.

There were signs, though, during 1964 that times might be changing. Terence Conran opened the first Habitat shop on the Fulham Road in London to politely suggest that houses need not reek of Fifties austerity but could instead resemble the sets of Scandinavian porn films. The Vietnam War was raging, and Lenny Bruce was imprisoned following an obscenity trial. Robert Moog demonstrated his early synthesizer and Roald Dahl's *Charlie and the Chocolate Factory* hit the shops for the first time, giving a generation hope that they, too, could find a 'golden ticket' to lift them out of the postwar gloom.

Of course there were wildly experimental musicians at work and play. Philip Glass was still studying on a scholarship in Paris but the German maverick Karlheinz Stockhausen had been busy on his eccentric, compelling works since the Fifties, and in 1964 released *Kontakte*. Karlheinz, it has to be said, was always going to be unlikely to trouble the charts unless he hooked up with a guaranteed hitmaker like Pete Waterman and formed a production company called Stockhausen and Waterman. However, if he sounded very little like The Beatles then by the time they got to piecing together 'Revolution 9' for what was known as 'The White Album' (released in 1968), The Beatles certainly sounded a bit like him.

Another giant of minimalism, New Yorker Steve Reich released the hypnotic *Music for two or more pianos*, and though John Cage didn't actually release anything in 1964, he was putting the finishing touches to *Variations IV*, which would surface the following year. Meanwhile, raised in a log cabin in Idaho and evidently obsessed with the sounds and silences of nature, La Monte Young chose 1964 to unveil *The Well-Tuned Piano*. Presumably a nod to Johann Sebastian Bach's *The Well-Tempered Clavier*, Young performed his piece on a Bösendorfer Imperial Grand, which spanned a complete eight octaves, giving the player an extra nine bass notes. The other intriguing point about the work is that it is intended to be ever evolving as, though there are a specified seven sections – divided into numerous subsections, and recognised themes – the score is more a work of philosophy or mathematics than traditional notation. There's plenty of room for improvisation and the loosest possible interpretation in there. To me it sounds like quite a tough listen as the strings of the piano, rather than being 'well tuned' are deliberately mistuned, and given that an average performance could last five to six hours, you have a challenging night out in prospect. There could easily be the feeling that the performance might never end, which is sort of how I felt as the Foo Fighters went into their third hour at Glastonbury in 2017.

Another of the genuine classics of minimalism also

sees the light of day in 1964 and that's Californian Terry Riley's *In C*. A selection of thirty-two phrases or melodic fragments, the musicians are encouraged to play them an arbitrary number of times. It is a work that continues to challenge and fascinate to this day and while my brief description of it might make it sound unlistenable, it is actually a thing of beauty and also, in contrast to *The Well-Tuned Piano*, can be over with in less than half an hour. Perhaps you'd be miffed if you'd bought a ticket and it was done that quickly. Personally, I'm fine with that: you can still have spaghetti carbonara and be home for nine. Ideal, but then my idea of a good night out is lunch. Perhaps the target audience for this is the boxing crowd. Admittedly the crossover between experimental music and pugilism is limited but those fans of Lord Queensberry's noble punch-ups seem happy to pay five hundred pounds for a ringside seat at a bout that lasts a matter of minutes. Having said all that, *In C*, given the arbitrariness of its duration, has been known to last nearly eighty minutes but that was when it was performed by the Terry Riley Repetition Orchestra. Well, you can't say you weren't warned.

So, though there was certainly sonic exploration going on in the first half of the Sixties, it had yet to really touch the world of rock. In 1964, we are still three years away from Jimi Hendrix's adventures with the electric guitar on *Are You Experienced* or Pink Floyd's psychedelic dreamscape *The Piper at the Gates of Dawn*, although only two years ahead of 'Tomorrow Never Knows' on The Beatles' *Revolver*.

So are The Beatles, on top of all their other well-documented achievements, the instigators of experimental rock? Well, yes. The first five seconds of 1964's 'I Feel Fine' make it the first piece of experimental music released on a major label and on a track that got to number one, no less. I know this sounds like an elaborately concocted claim, but the other pretenders to the crown are still on the nursery slopes. Perhaps if they'd spent less time skiing they'd have got albums out sooner.

In a way it's unsurprising, even this early on The Beatles had been intrigued by studio accidents such as stray talkback and tape glitches and the like, so an experimental seed was already planted. I had always assumed that those unexpected opening sounds had been produced by George Harrison on the Gretsch Tennessean he was playing at that time, but this turns out not to be the case. The first thudding note is from Paul McCartney's bass. The following four seconds of noise come from John Lennon's red sunburst Gibson J-160E, only the second electro-acoustic the company made, and still in production today. Evidently John had inadvertently left the guitar leaning on the amplifier with the volume turned up, creating the historic squall of noise. Immediately animated by the sound, he encouraged George Martin to make use of it and so Martin decided to edit it into the front of the track.

In 1975 Brian Eno, in collaboration with the artist Peter Schmidt, released a box of cards called *Oblique Strategies*, which we'll come back to later in this book. These were enigmatic instructions that you selected from the pack at random, and which you should resort to if you found yourself at an impasse with whatever you were working on. You are not encouraged to overthink these gnomic directives but to just absorb them and see where they take you. I have my set here now – in a box signed by Brian, as I am in showbusiness – and I'll pick three at random now to give you a flavour:

1. Don't stress one thing more than another.

2. Disconnect from desire.

3. Take a break.

Okay, well, I can't stress enough how much I value the advice of Eno so, having picked 'take a break' at random, I have no option other than to follow the directive and so I'm going to sign off for a bit and have a cup of tea and come back after a blank page. See you in a bit.

This page intentionally left blank*

---

* Except it's not because it's got this on it!

Hi, I'm back now. Also amongst those cards are four that would seem to encapsulate how the first five seconds of 'I Feel Fine' came about. One is perhaps the most oft-quoted: 'Honor thy error as a hidden intention', followed by 'Emphasize the flaws' and 'Give way to your worst impulse'. All these would seem to apply here as does the fourth: 'Ask people to work against their better judgement', which seems to be exactly what Lennon did with George Martin.

This moment of seemingly musical happenstance is followed by a wave of sonic divergence. Getting underway in 1966 are Frank Zappa and The Mothers of Invention with *Freak Out!*. Inevitably, as the 1967 Summer of Love sweeps the globe, key records appear. Gong are only just coalescing in Paris, but Captain Beefheart's *Safe as Milk* comes out, as does *The Velvet Underground & Nico*. Amon Düül don't unleash *Psychedelic Underground* until 1969, when Can also get cracking with *Monster Movie*. Kraftwerk's first release comes the following year.

But what of The Beatles themselves? After the break-up of the band was officially announced in April 1970, did this nascent experimentalism manifest itself in their solo careers? Both released that spring, Ringo and Paul's solo releases of *Sentimental Journey* and *McCartney* respectively (in case you thought *McCartney* was by Starr), were traditional song-based records and pretty much exactly what you'd expect. In fact, Macca doesn't make any remotely experimental music, not that he's under any obligation to, of course, until the

Nineties when he began his project, The Fireman, with producer Youth. George's case is interesting. His first post-Beatles release was *All Things Must Pass*, a triple album no less, perhaps a way of telling us he had all these songs but those other two herberts wouldn't use any of them. However, he did make two albums while still in the group: the instrumental film soundtrack *Wonderwall Music* in 1968 and *Electronic Sound* the following year, played exclusively on the synthesizer that Robert Moog had been demonstrating at the time of 'I Feel Fine'.

Perhaps predictably, given his restlessness, truculence and marriage to the conceptual artist Yoko Ono, John's early solo works were adventurous to say the least. Released in 1968 and 1969 amidst the chaotic dissolution of The Beatles, *Unfinished Music No. 1: Two Virgins*, *Unfinished Music No. 2: Life with the Lions* and *Wedding Album* are certainly avant-garde, though not necessarily in a good way. To be fair, rather like Terry Riley's Repetition Orchestra, you can't accuse Lennon of leaving you surprised as to what you're about to get. Though a perfectly natural reaction on hearing *Unfinished Music 1* or *2* is to say, 'Well, finish it then and come back to me when it's done.' To give you a flavour: *Life with the Lions* includes a track called 'No Bed for Beatle John' which is made of up of John and Yoko reading out clips from the newspapers about themselves when they were in Queen Charlotte's Hospital following Ono's miscarriage. However, his first solo album proper, post-Fabs, is the majestic song collection to be found on *Imagine*.

It's tempting, then, to think that, for the Fab Four, the experimental urge that begins with 'I Feel Fine' and triumphantly bears full fruit on 'Tomorrow Never Knows' and *Sgt. Pepper's Lonely Hearts Club Band*, was an itch best scratched from within the security of the band, from where they could have combined experimentation with commercial success indefinitely and created a baton for other musicians to pick up and run with. Keen to break free of the shackles of Beatledom though they were, avant-gardism was no basis for a solo career: it would have seemed foolhardy to painstakingly build such a reputation only to demolish it with albums of self-indulgent junk. As another *Oblique Strategies* card has it: 'Slow preparation . . . Fast execution.'

9

House Party

In the town where I live, Knutsford in Cheshire, May Day is a massive deal. In fact, it can officially proclaim itself to be 'Royal May Day' as King Edward VII and Queen Alexandra, the then Prince and Princess of Wales, bestowed the honour in 1887. In a tradition going back to 1864, on the first Saturday of the month there is a huge parade in lavish costume through the streets ending up on the Heath where there are many municipal events and a huge funfair. The town teems with life as revellers and May-ers jostle for a view of proceedings and, as the day wears on, stagger from pub to pub.

Just around the corner from my house is a hostelry called The Legh Arms where music events are staged fairly regularly. May Day 2019 was no exception as an evening of DJ sets was advertised. What many locals strolling past may not have realised was that they were about to have a genuine legend of house music in . . .

ermmm . . . the house. For one of the DJs billed was Marshall Jefferson. A pioneer of house music and beats while resident in Chicago, in 'Move Your Body' he created perhaps the definitive break-out track of the genre and helped to create a worldwide phenomenon. And he was coming to spin discs at my local boozer. Amazing.

Jefferson has in fact lived in the northwest of England for some time, having been drawn to Manchester initially by the demands for his services at the Hacienda night-club. Such is the myth and sense of awe that now surrounds Manchester's Hacienda, when young whipper-snappers ask if I ever went there and I reply in the affirmative, they look at me as if I've been to the moon. 'And what was it like?' they ask, wide-eyed in expecta-tion, to which I reply, 'More or less empty, freezing cold and with terrible sound.' They think I'm joking, as my DJ career has given me the reputation as something of a japester and I was in fact cringingly described by the newspaper of the town of my birth as 'the Boltonion funster'. That sums me up perfectly. Next time my wife expresses frustration or disappointment at my moods or actions I'll be sure to remind her that funster is my default settting.

However, as is often the case, I'm not joking. I'm old enough to remember the Hac in its previous incarnation as those premises formerly held that most vital of city centre facilities: a yacht sales room. Admittedly the canal network oozed nearby but I don't recall ever seeing anyone crack a bottle of Pomagne over the bow, hoist the mainsail, don the old captain's hat and set off for the Manchester Ship Canal. Not quite the same as drifting around the Cyclades, is it?

When Factory opened the club in 1982, it seemed a bold – even foolhardy – move. And as it turned out, it was both. The city centre was a much darker place than today's glittering metropolis of glass and chrome. The Hacienda's location on Whitworth Street West took you away from the comparatively bright lights of Oxford Road and out towards the shadowy extremities. At the time I was presenting an indie music show on local station Piccadilly Radio called *Transmission*. The show was named partly in tribute to the Joy Division song of the same name, and accordingly I had a close relationship with the bods at Factory Records and the wonderfully enthusiastic, enigmatic and often pretentious newshound and new sounds nut Tony Wilson.

At one of our regular meetings, he gave me a black and yellow plastic membership card for this new discotheque that he said was going to revolutionise Manchester's nightlife. My memory is that my card had membership number fourteen on it. Or it could have been sixteen. Naturally, not being one of life's hoarders, that card is long gone but, boy, do I wish I'd kept it as I could now have sold it to some Manc memorabilia magpie for the price of a package holiday.

Tony's dream of a packed dancefloor with the latest sounds emanating from the DJ booth would eventually become a reality and not just for groovers of the north-west. Ravers came from right across the country, or indeed from across the pond in the case of Marshall

Jefferson, to sample its unique atmosphere. It had a unique atmosphere in the early days too, though not in a positive way. As I stood one night watching Sandie Shaw singing – though such was the echoey nature of the acoustics that I can't be sure what she was singing – and pulled my reefer jacket more tightly around me to keep warm, I thought it would never work. In fact, ultimately it didn't as Peter Hook explains at length in his book, *The Hacienda: How Not to Run a Club*. Following repeated drug busts and the presence of weaponry, the club closed its doors in 1997.

Being more of a lark than an owl, I've never been much of a clubber really. This despite my utter worship of the owl. I mean, what a beast of mystery, beauty and charisma. What other creature can turn its head two hundred and seventy degrees each way – except for that projectile vomiting girl in the film *The Exorcist*? By comparison, the lark is an unremarkable-looking fellow, though it does have a reputation as a fine singer and is mentioned both in Chaucer's *Canterbury Tales* – in 'The Knight's Tale' – and in Shakespeare's Sonnets where it is invoked as the harbinger of dawn.

I used to work for the now defunct BBC Radio One in partnership with Marc Riley, the artist formerly known as Lard. Occasionally we would find ourselves involved in some station shenanigans over a weekend away somewhere, which involved keeping the hours of vampires, accompanied by a throbbing beat and overpriced drinks. Marc and I hit on the perfect plan of heading out on the town around six or seven and having a meal and a bottle of Pinot Noir before heading to that night's big club venue and making sure everyone had seen us. We would then scoot back to the budget hotel and enjoy a quick nightcap, retiring by midnight. We would set the alarm for about seven the following morning and, donning the same clothes we'd had on the night before, make for the appointed chill-out room where we were pronounced 'hardcore' by Fabio or possibly Grooverider. We, like them, had done an all-nighter. It's just that ours had involved seven hours' kip.

Despite cutting quite the dash in my white cheesecloth shirt with embroidered heart and elasticated waist, coupled with pristine purple flares that meticulously covered my platform shoes even when I gyrated to The Four Seasons' 'December, 1963 (Oh, What A Night)' at the Nocturne in Bolton in the mid-Seventies, my clubbing days were short-lived. Unsurprisingly then, I never made a pilgrimage to the club that claims to have been the birthplace of house music. And even if I'd been so inclined, I wouldn't have had the air fare to Chicago at the time.

Musically, Chicago is a city that has been home to many movements, but the most significant came with the Great Migration, which lasted from 1916 to 1970, during which time six million African Americans left the Southern States in search of a better way of life and standard of living. In the census of 1910, 90 per cent of African Americans were shown to be living in the South. By the time the migration was deemed to be over, that figure had dropped to 50 per cent. Accordingly, the major cities were swamped with incomers bringing their musical passions – in particular jazz and blues. Blues giants like Howlin' Wolf, Muddy Waters and Sonny Boy Williamson made the city of Chicago their home – as did jazz and swing greats Nat King Cole and Louis Armstrong. Admittedly, the sound of Louis Armstrong and His Hot Five was pure New Orleans Dixieland, but they recorded everything at the studios of OKeh Records in Chicago.

The city also forged a reputation for quality soft soul and funk. This was largely built on the success of a band from Chattanooga, Tennessee, called The Impressions whose members included a young Curtis Mayfield. Their success and signing to ABC-Paramount Records in 1961 instigated a move to the Windy City and many other hit artists would find it a secure base from which to operate. The great Sam Cooke was born in Clarksdale but had lived in Chicago since he was a toddler. The Chi-Lites, The Staple Singers, Earth, Wind & Fire, Rufus and Chaka Khan all operated from the same streets down the years and became global stars. Oh and there was that band who sang 'If You Leave Me Now'. Oh, what were they called? I'm sure they were from Chicago. (Note to self: look this up later.)

House music was born at, and named after, a Chicago club called the Warehouse, which operated from 1977 to 1983 and whose resident DJ was Frankie Knuckles. He evidently didn't realise that house music was even a thing until he saw a sign in a South Side bar that proclaimed: 'We play house music.' They were obviously keen to get punters through the door and must have witnessed Frankie's ability to pack a venue and dance-floor with his trademark trick of extending mixes and tracks with reel-to-reel tape and drum machines to really emphasise the beats.

And the beats were all important. The music was in 4/4 and was minimalistic, repetitive and beat heavy, which is just what you want if you're pumped up and fuelled on a sweaty dancefloor. And as house records began to be made, certain beat sounds became central to the genre. These were provided by the Roland TR-808 drum machine, from whence 808 State took their name, which was produced between 1980 and 1983. Now seen as one of the key devices in the history of recorded music, it was somewhat derided on its launch for the unrealistic drum sounds it spewed out. Well, fair enough, but it did create a whole new rhythmic soundscape, and if you want the sound of real drums you always have the option of hiring a real drummer.

So pursuit of the perfect beat became all-consuming to the extent that on some house records the beat was pretty much all there was. Minimalism was, of course, nothing new and there had been several notable records – and in some cases hits – which were stripped back to their bare bones to compelling effect. German band Trio had a monster hit in 1982 with 'Da Da Da', a song driven by the chirruping beat of the Casio VL-Tone, a mono synth you could fit in your pocket. The early Eighties also brought a different type of minimalist recording that consisted of voice, ambience and not much else: Jane's 'It's a Fine Day' and 'There Goes Concorde Again' by . . . And the Native Hipsters. Going back further to 1970 there is plenty going on in James Brown's 'Funky Drummer' but extended versions break down to the pure beat played by Clyde Stubblefield.

For consumers and artists who had been used to songs committed to record being multitracked and meticulously produced, the stripped-back brutality of these various recordings was initially hard to embrace. There is, of course, an argument that you will never appreciate tracks like these unless you are at the right club at the right time of night having ingested the right drugs. Having said that, the discussion about how minimal a piece can be, and what constitutes music, pre-dates house by decades. The Los Angeles-born venerated minimalist composer John Cage published a work entitled '4'33"' in 1952. It is a work in three movements for any instrument or combination of instruments. And it consists of . . . nothing. It is twenty-seven seconds shy of being five minutes of silence. Apparently Cage had become increasingly irritated by the bland Muzak that was piped into every lift and shopping mall and thought it would be an epic wheeze to sell the company a piece which constituted a break in transmission. A pause for thought. And there is something in that, for sure. As Norwegian explorer and adventurer Erling Kagge says in his book *Silence: In the Age of Noise*: 'that which is soundless within you remains a mystery'. And we can all do with a bit of mystery in our lives, right?

John Cage was also inspired by the 1951 'White

Paintings' of his friend Robert Rauschenberg. These are, as the name suggests, canvases of plain white but when the light changes throughout the day, the surfaces, Cage noted, 'caught whatever fell on them'. The same year, Cage visited Harvard University's anechoic chamber. This is a facility so acoustically insulated that pure silence is possible. However, John claimed that when left in this oppressive box he could in fact hear a high and low hum. The engineer told him the high sound was his nervous system at work and the low his blood circulating. I don't know if this is true, but it certainly makes you wonder if absolute silence is something any of us will ever experience.

John Cage had studied Zen Buddhism and so there was certainly some sort of meditative aim with '4'33"'. Sitting in front of one of Rauschenburg's canvases, you could enter a trance-like state. I know people who claim to have the same experience when viewing Mark Rothko's work. Cage wanted the audience to sit and observe and contemplate and accept the notion that sounds can be music.

The debut performance of the work took place at the appropriately named Maverick Concert Hall in Woodstock on 29 August 1952. David Tudor, a pianist and composer of experimental music himself, sat onstage at a piano and opened, then later closed, the lid to signify the beginnings and ends of the three movements.

In 2010, in a bizarre twist to the story of the most minimalistic piece ever recorded, a Facebook campaign was launched to make it a Christmas number one in the

UK. Those were the times when with dreary predictability the winner of *The X Factor* routinely nabbed that pop honour. Irritated by this, a group of pranksters launched a campaign to get four and a half minutes of silence to the top slot. In the end, though '4'33"' did chart at number twenty-one, *X Factor*'s inexorable march to the top continued, and that year's winner Matt Cardle became the 2010 Christmas number one.

Marshall Jefferson may not have performed '4'33"' but he did spend a lot of time in front of a piano. If the Roland drum machines and bass synths gave house its characteristic sounds, it was Marshall who added the distinctive and influential piano. In 2018 Jefferson paid a visit to the studios of the BBC 6Music show I co-present with Stuart Maconie, and he told us that the creation of that unmistakable and much copied sound was a painstaking process. Unable to play the piano – always a drawback when playing one, perhaps except for if you're doing '4'33"' – he had to slow the tracks down until he was able to create the chords one note at a time. His classic track, 'Move Your Body', which became a Hacienda favourite, was released in 1986 and was the first house record ever released.

Or was it? There are those who say that the first key recorded work came in 1982 with Charanjit Singh's album *Synthesizing: Ten Ragas to a Disco Beat*, and others who say Jesse Saunders and Vince Lawrence nailed it in 1983 with 'On and On'. Mr Fingers released 'Mystery of Love' in 1985, the same year that Chip E, or Larry to his mates, dropped 'It's House'. But Marshall's

tune was the first one to break out of the house fraternity and take the clubs of the world by storm. It was a
guaranteed dancefloor filler which, at the Hacienda, was
something I thought I would never see.

10

To the Manor Born

As I was saying when describing the location of the Hacienda, Manchester in the mid-Seventies could be a dark and forbidding place, certainly if you ventured off the main drags into the sepulchral alleys and back streets.

When I started my job at Piccadilly Radio, I had to park my rusting Renault on a litter-infested wasteland of asphalt and walk through the narrow Dickensian streets, home to multitudinous rag-trade sweat shops, to make my way to the radio station. Piccadilly Radio was wedged in a half floor underneath the concrete castle of the Piccadilly Hotel and above the static electricity generating substation trading as Brentford Nylons, for whom noted disc jockey Alan 'Fluff' Freeman once did a television advert promoting their sheets at only one pound sixty-nine. Given the lack of comfort and shock potential they brought, that still looks expensive to me – and remember that one pound sixty-nine then is equivalent to a thousand pounds in today's money. It's not really, but nylon bed sheets were an abomination which, when coupled with nylon pyjamas, could potentially result in you jumping into bed on one side and sliding straight out the other with only your friction burns for company.

At the end of the working day, tired not least from the four pints of Tetley's bitter supped by me and everyone else during the lunch break, I made the same sun-starved sojourn back through the grimy ginnels to see if my car was still where I had left it. To be honest, I was always fairly confident it would be, on the basis that it wasn't worth stealing, though you could never be absolutely sure. A friend of mine shuffled through the shadows to discover that his powder blue MG Midget had vanished. Closer inspection revealed that it was in fact still there but had been upended onto its side meaning that only the undercarriage was visible, or indeed not initially visible in the Mancunian murk. I mean, what was the point in someone having done that? Mindless vandalism is one thing but that must have taken a good deal of effort on the part of the miscreants. It never happened to me, but I did once return to find a phalanx of gentlemen-of-the-road leaning against my car while toasting themselves, and some dubious sausages, by a large campfire. I informed them that their backrest was soon to be on the move, though this was by no means a certainty given the state of the engine. They replied in a barely decipherable lingo that that wasn't especially convenient for them, but would I like to hang on until the bangers were done and gnaw at one in their whiffy company? Enticing invitation though this was, I politely declined and stopped for steak pudding and chips on the way home before inadvertently dropping my car and house keys down a grid on Mauldeth Road. Ah, happy days.

Occasionally on these twilight strolls I would encounter a tall, gaunt, bald individual in dark clothing lurking in a Newton Street doorway. He looked a bit like a dishevelled Mckon from the Dan Dare comic strip or the subject of Edvard Munch's *The Scream*. Despite his rather forbidding appearance, I eventually discovered he was an affable cove called Richard Boon and he was the Buzzcocks' manager. The great and gregarious Tony Wilson was of course one of the main enablers of the Manchester scene but Richard Boon also played a key part. First, Buzzcocks not only invited the Sex Pistols to town to kick-start punk in the northwest of England, but thanks to the sadly now late Pete Shelley, also created a catalogue of fantastic songs. Rather like the Ramones, Buzzcocks enthusiastically embraced punk, sawing their guitars in half and playing two-note guitar solos, but realised too that, though the fans demanded energy and danger, they also wanted pop music you could sing along to while gobbing and pogoing. And has there ever been a finer pop song than 'Ever Fallen in Love'?

Even more important than that single, however, was their debut *Spiral Scratch* EP of January 1977. It was recorded in three hours, with another two set aside for mixing. The total cost of the session and manufacture of the record was five hundred pounds or two hundred and ninety-five bed sheets from Brentford Nylons in old money. The studio was alien territory to the band and their utter naivety showed when they thought you had to pause and stay quiet between takes, because that's how it sounded between tracks on records. They were, in effect, recording their own silences between the songs. Bless. Crucially, however, it was released on New Hormones, which was their own label, making them the first British punk band to release their music independently. The idea that four scruffy scallywags from our own city could put their own record out without going down to that there London to look for a deal was absolutely mind-blowing, and hugely empowering. Like Tony always said, 'We don't need anyone from London to give us permission to do it.'

The self-belief that that gave music makers and fans in Manchester like me cannot be overstated and certainly gave me the confidence to hanker and beg for my own radio show as it seemed only right that the local station should feature the local talent. Rather surprisingly, in 1980 the powers-that-be agreed and gave me a slot on Saturday afternoons over the summer months when there was no football being played. They told me I could play whatever I liked as long as I carried the cricket scores from the local leagues which was fine by me. I was absolutely thrilled. The atmosphere in the Manchester music scene at that time was so creative and bursting with energy and excitement that I was just delighted to have my place in it. And of course I found myself in a role I would occupy on various stations for the whole of my working life to date. I'm not sure that would ever have happened but for the inspirational characters and artists from those heady Manc days of yore.

Sadly, *Spiral Scratch* cannot claim to be the first punk record released to express a bit of anarchy in the UK. Nor was it the Pistols' 'Anarchy in the UK', which came out in November 1976 on major label EMI. Similarly, The Clash sold themselves to CBS and opened their account with 'White Riot' in February 1977, a month after that Buzzcocks debut release. The generally accepted winners of the race to release the first new-wave single are The Damned, who not only unleashed 'New Rose' in October of 1976, but also 'did the right thing' by putting it out on an independent label in the shape of Stiff Records. Buzzcocks can still claim the true indie bragging rights, however, as their label was their own, funded only by money they'd begged and borrowed themselves. Nobody else was backing them and so you can make a case for that being the first indie release of those pioneering times.

In point of fact, trying to pinpoint the first independent labels and recordings ever made is more or less impossible: we have to go way back before Stiff was founded in 1976 – Factory and Rough Trade joined the party in 1978 – to days when records were on labels that barely existed. You could even make a case for the birth of indie labels happening way back in the Delta blues days of the Thirties when a label could be launched just to release a single record.

The word 'indie' is also problematic in itself. For many years it came to mean rough-edged music played on guitars by bedraggled guttersnipes of no fixed hairstyle. Recently the definition has broadened as it certainly should, as 'indie' music could be any style as long as it's produced without the help of a major corporation. In theory you could be an indie band signed to the behemoth Universal which makes barely any sense at all. Certainly, though indie generally equated to scruffy, the first independent labels to really make an impact were anything but unkempt. Berry Gordy launched Tamla Records, and then Motown in Detroit in 1959, with Stax coming out of Memphis two years later, and their artists had to be immaculately turned out. Staying with Memphis, Sam Phillips started trading as Sun Records as early as 1950, releasing records by the likes of Elvis Presley, Carl Perkins, Johnny Cash and Jerry Lee Lewis.

For obvious reasons, some seminal indie labels later became, or were taken over by, large companies. A notable example of this is Island, which Chris Blackwell co-founded in Jamaica in 1959 and was bought by Polygram in 1989. Taking his company's name from the Harry Belafonte hit 'Island in the Sun', Blackwell was keen to commit the glorious reggae vibes he was hearing every day to vinyl, and it is in fact reggae that connects us to the single most extraordinary business trajectory of one particular independent label. It might seem difficult to think of the Virgin name now as anything but a major corporation but it was once a watchword for a brave new world of music and free thinking. The love of reggae it shared with Island, and its desire to make those sounds available to the ordinary music fan, being a case in point.

If you were a thrusting young musical adventurer in Manchester in the late Seventies, and I like to think I was, you would have beeen drawn inexorably to Virgin Records on Lever Street. I know. It's amazing, isn't it? Virgin? Surely not the same Virgin as money and airlines and spaceships and island retreats for billionaires? Yes, that Virgin. It began under the auspices of a young, vaguely hippieish Richard Branson as Virgin Records and Tapes at Notting Hill Gate, where it provided vegetarian food and bean bags to sit on. With a logo created by that acclaimed archbishop of art to the royalty of prog-rock Roger Dean, the operation was christened 'Virgin' as Branson and his team of like-minded mates were all business 'virgins'. They opened their first proper outlet above a shoe shop on Tottenham Court Road. Their link to Island came in 1978 when the subsidiary imprint Virgin Front Line was forged in collaboration with Blackwell's organisation and began to release quite brilliant compilations of reggae tunes, enabling us to hear such greats as U-Roy, The Mighty Diamonds, Peter Tosh, Culture, Gregory Isaacs and Prince Far-I for the first time, as you could pick these albums up at budget prices. In fact, price point was central to the launch of Virgin: one of their first releases was *The Faust Tapes* by Faust, which had a retail price of forty-nine pence or just over a third of a Brentford Nylons sheet. It is also accepted wisdom that Gong's *Camembert Électrique* was on Virgin, costing a hefty fifty-nine pence. Actually, it originally came out on the French label BYG Actuel in 1971, though it was reissued under licence to Branson in 1974. However, their 1973 long player *Flying Teapot* was indeed released by the natty narcissist of Necker Island and gave him the idea for Virgin Airlines. Possibly.

In the late Seventies, a decade and a half before Virgin was sold to EMI for a reputed five hundred million pounds – enough to furnish two hundred and ninety-five million beds at a certain well-known electrostatically infused bedding outlet – the Virgin shop in Manchester was where you hung out to meet and chat with people you'd met at gigs and hear the new sounds being blasted over the in-store speakers. The manager of the time also helped out Richard Boon, whose office was in the next street, by stocking *Spiral Scratch* and encouraging other regional stores to do the same. So Virgin as a company was run with very much an independent spirit, embodied by the first album they put out on the label.

Tubular Bells came out in May 1973 as its creator Mike Oldfield was a callow youth just turning twenty. Nevertheless, he had a seasoned track record as a musician. Despite being a big fan of Hank Marvin, like everyone else in England who had a guitar in the Sixties, he went down the folk route and was an habitué of the clubs around Reading, where he performed in several guises, including a duo with his singing sister Sally (they were actually signed to the prestigious Transatlantic label). By 1970 he was in The Whole World, who played with Kevin Ayers, and this was when he met keyboardist and arranger David Bedford, who not only encouraged Mike to work on the embryonic fragments that would crystallise into his masterpiece but would later be at the helm for its orchestral realisation. Oldfield might have seemed to be at a precocious age to be mixing in such vaunted company but you have to remember that life expectancy was a lot lower back then as you had been pre-programmed to work, draw your state pension for four or five years and then snuff it so as not to bankrupt the nation. There was none of this eighty-year-olds-running-the-London-Marathon nonsense. So musicians, like everyone else, had to pack a lot in early on.

In the early Seventies Richard Branson had acquired Shipton Manor in Oxfordshire with the help of a £30,000 loan from an aunt. I don't know about you, but I've never had any aunts like that, though my Aunty Mary did used to make amazing potato cakes. A state-of-the-art recording studio was duly installed at the manor and one of the early engineers was Tom Newman. Newman soon befriended the young Oldfield who was there to record sessions for other artists on guitar and bass. As their relationship strengthened the reticent Mike began to play snatches of what would become *Tubular Bells* to Tom, who insisted he return home and bring back all the demos he had. Convinced of its potential, he persuaded Richard to give them one week's studio time to see if the project would come to anything.

Embarking on this was no mean feat, as barring a few minor musical roles, Oldfield was playing everything himself from the opening Steinway Grand Piano to the eponymous bells themselves, which were already present, having been hired in for a previous session by John Cale. It is said that the sound achieved using the mallets provided didn't satisfy the young maestro and so he eventually finished up clobbering them with a builder's claw hammer, breaking one of the tubes. The presence of Viv Stanshall, whose sonorous voice famously introduces a succession of instruments at the end of part one, was due to him turning up early for the following week's session at which the Bonzo Dog Doo-Dah Band were starting out on another album. It can be said, then, that *Tubular Bells* is, in many ways, the first truly 'solo' album of all time, as Oldfield pretty much composed and performed it all on his own. Eventually, Mike and Tom got it into one piece, Virgin released it and seemingly nearly everyone under the age of twenty-five bought a copy. With sales of around two million, seven hundred thousand, it is the forty-fourth biggest selling album in the UK at the time of writing, one above Travis's *The Man Who* and one below *Parachutes* by Coldplay.*

---

* I was surprised to see that all three of these records had outsold ABBA's *Greatest Hits* (1976), which lies down there at number forty-seven, until I realised that the notably similarly titled *ABBA Gold: Greatest Hits* (1992) is up there at number two just under Queen's *Greatest Hits*, which is the only artefact to have sold more than six million – although if ABBA had had one and not two compilations they might have snatched victory from Freddie and co. Then again, Queen's *Greatest Hits Volume II* also props up the top ten and so . . . oh well, I don't know. You do the maths.

In 1992 Mike Oldfield released a long-awaited follow-up in *Tubular Bells II*. A spectacular concert performance was arranged for Edinburgh Castle with all the drama that setting inevitably brings. I went up there to interview the inspirational instrumentalist and being a bit of a poptastic pranketeer, broadcasting buffoon and dickhead DJ, my opening gambit was:

> 'Well, Mike, it must have taken you ages to come up with the title.'

To which his response was:

> 'Yes, listeners, the next sound you will hear is me punching him in the face.'

And who can blame him? I'd do it differently now, though he was gracious enough to do the whole interview as planned. I mean, really, how dare I? I was a bloke off the radio and he was a genius who revolutionised solo recording and released one of the most important indie records ever made. Sorry, Mike.

11

The Single Life

In a sense, there is little to say about either Eddy Arnold or 'Texarkana Baby' though I'll tell you what you need to know presently. So how does this record constitute a crossroads moment? Simple. It was the first forty-five rpm seven-inch vinyl single ever released, and as discs in that format have been the lifeblood of rock and roll, whether being bought to spin at home, blasting out from the world's jukeboxes or making up the all-important Top Twenty, the first one ever issued is a major landmark in our story.

Immediately, however, there's a caveat. I say the vinyl single is the 'lifeblood of rock and roll', but that statement is undermined by the fact that the best-selling example is the distinctly un-rock and roll 'White Christmas' by Bing Crosby. Released in 1942 it has sold over fifty million copies, although technically some of those must have been released on other formats as the forty-five rpm single wasn't invented in 1942. However,

Bing is also in this chart of charts at number three with 'Silent Night', on thirty million copies sold. Great tracks though they are, they are hardly the stuff to spark thrusting urges of adolescent rebellion, so what's at number two?

Unfortunately sandwiched between two Bings, which you suspect in his wild younger days might have been a good night out for Elton, is Mister John himself with his reworking of 'Candle in the Wind' to commemorate the death of Princess Diana. That's sold over thirty-three million copies. Whitney Houston is at five having clocked up twenty million sales of 'I Will Always Love You' and so, at number four, with twenty-five million copies, it is left to Bill Haley – the tubby tartan-jacketed, kiss-curled Comet king – to set teenage toes a-tapping with 'Rock Around the Clock'.

But the pure essence of pop and rock is held on a seven-inch disc. Admittedly, most of us will be able to recall the first album we ever bought, but as singles were cheaper and more affordable with newspaper-round wages or pocket money, that would have been where it all began. And there was a magic to buying your very first disc. A feeling of electricity crackled through you at point of purchase. For many years when asked about the first record I ever bought I routinely said it was 'Virginia Plain' by Roxy Music, released in 1972 when I was fourteen. So that sounds plausible and shows remarkably good taste for a whey-faced youth. And I did buy that record. I can remember vividly getting it from Boots the Chemists in Bolton.

However, round the corner from Boots, just near the Market Hall, was an electrical retailer called Derek Guest's. They had a gramophone department and I have an equally vivid memory of going there and buying a horrifically naff hit by Melbourne band The Mixtures called 'The Pushbike Song'. As I recollect, my brother was bought 'Blame It On the Pony Express' by Johnny Johnson and the Bandwagon on the same outlandish spree. As both of these were released in 1970 I must have erased this from my recall subconsciously, or possibly consciously, in order to make myself look like quite the trainee hipster when forging a carapace of cool in which to cocoon myself as I began my ascent of the DJ mountain. Or maybe, and I admit I'm clutching at straws here, those records were bought for us as a treat by my parents and so 'Virginia Plain' was the first one I bought myself after all. So, as I say, everybody remembers the first single they bought. Except me, apparently.

The forty-five rpm seven-inch vinyl disc with a track on each side was actually launched by RCA Victor in 1949. Before that, records tended to be ten inches in diameter and play at seventy-eight, which was the format of Bing's multi-million-selling 'White Christmas' during the Forties. They were also pressed in a compound in which shellac was a major constituent. Shellac was not only brittle but relatively hard to come by, being secreted by the female lac bug onto trees in the forests of India and Thailand. And I'm not making this up. I suppose in a sense it's no weirder than ambergris, basically hardened sperm whale puke, being used in the production of perfume. A bloke walking his dog on the beach in Morecambe recently found a lump of what perfumiers refer to as 'floating gold' and flogged it for one hundred thousand pounds. To put that windfall in perspective, I just checked on RightMove where estate agents Farrell Heyworth are offering a very tidy, stone-built, four bedroomed three-storey house on Central Drive in Morecambe for ninety-nine thousand, nine hundred and fifty pounds. So, man walks dog. Finds lump of old vomit (or it could be poo, nobody seems too sure). Cashes in to the tune of a new gaff. Not bad, eh?

In the Fifties the battle of the speeds raged as RCA Victor pressed on with their forty-fives, while their biggest competitor, Columbia, went down the twelve-inch thirty-three-and-a-third route. Record sales had grown massively in post-Depression America but now discs were becoming cheaper and a lot more robust. If you dropped your prized shellac recording, it would shatter into a hundred pieces and the secreting efforts of the Thai ladybugs were in vain. If you dropped your new vinyl single you still had something playable. Eventually we would reach the wonders of the indestructible, or so we were led to believe, compact disc era. Perhaps you remember the launch during which it was stated that you could spread jam on on a CD and it would still play. Yes, two things: 1. Why would you? And 2. It wouldn't.

RCA's launch of the seven-inch was nothing if not imaginative. They used a colour coding for different genres of music, much like the crew of the *USS*

Enterprise had their roles identified. Captain James T. Kirk and his buddies in Command wore yellow, while scientific and medical staff donned blue, with operations and engineering bods swathed in bright red. I've always liked this idea and rather wish it could have been rolled out at the BBC where I've spent most of my working life. How much simpler it would have been to tell what everyone was doing if engineers had worn purple, journalists puce, management shit brown and us glamorous disc jockeys shimmering silver lamé or something similarly glittery to mark us out from civilians.

RCA Victor also went to the trouble of releasing different kinds of music on different coloured vinyl. 'Popular' music was on black, childrens' on yellow, classical on red, gospel and R&B on orange, with operettas and 'semi-classical' on midnight blue. Oh, and Country on green which we'll come to in a moment.

Technically, the very first single ever released was a demonstration record spelling out the benefits of this new technology, which was dubbed 'remarkably faithful' by the great orchestral maestro Arturo Toscanini. We are reassured by the narrator on this disc that there are 'no breakage worries'. We're also told that one hundred and fifty records, that will fit into 'one small foot of bookshelf space', will bring twenty-four hours of listening pleasure. This figure bothered me and so I did some sums. If your average single has a three-minute song on each side, that's six minutes multiplied by one hundred and fifty which is nine hundred. Dividing this by sixty minutes would give you fifteen hours of listening pleasure.

Admittedly, you could listen to some of them again but in that case one single could in theory give you twenty-four hours of listening pleasure. But perhaps I do them a disservice. Maybe they were cramming much longer tracks onto these meagre discs.

And how much can you get on a seven-inch anyway? John Lennon and George Martin were concerned about a lack of sound quality with 'Hey Jude' in 1968 which clocked in at seven minutes and eleven seconds. The basis of their worry was that if you try and get too much music onto a vinyl disc there would be a degradation in sound quality and volume as the grooves are cut narrower and closer together. In actual fact, though, they had been beaten to the longest single milestone earlier the same year when Richard Harris's 'MacArthur Park' trumped them by nine seconds. However, Bruce Springsteen can beat that. The B-side of The Boss's 1987 live single 'Fire', when released in the US, was a song called 'Incident on 57th Street' on stage with The E Street Band. This has a duration of just over ten minutes, all crammed on to seven-inch vinyl and playing at forty-five rpm.

I suppose you could say that to rightfully hold the title of longest single ever it really ought to be an A-side, which means that Laurie Anderson's 'O Superman' from 1981 comes into play at eight minutes and twenty-one seconds. A decade earlier, however, The Who issued 'Won't Get Fooled Again' as a single from their *Who's Next* album, which is a bit of a classic despite having one of the worst covers of all time. The feeble pun of the album title is pictorialised by the members of the band zipping up their flies having urinated on a concrete monolith. Or four pillocks pissing on a pillar if you like. 'Won't Get Fooled Again' runs to eight minutes and twenty-eight seconds which I certainly used to enjoy to the full as I gobbled a pasty in the cafeteria of Manchester University Students' Union knowing I had maximised the cash I'd inserted into the jukebox. However, I now see that The Who only ever released an edit of this track as a single so it must have been the album version that echoed round that refectory. You're probably wondering about 'Bohemian Rhapsody' here too, but amazingly, despite its different sections and operatic aspirations, it clocks in at under six minutes. The longest single I can actually find is 'November Rain' by Guns N' Roses, which clocks in at eight minutes and fifty-three seconds of histrionic caterwauling and top-hatted guitar posturing.

The jukebox and the single was, of course, a marriage made in heaven and immortalised in every film and TV show set in the Fifties or early Sixties. Hepcats and beatniks would gather round said machine to grin inanely and click their fingers to the latest sounds thumping through that big bass speaker. The coin-operated phonograph had actually been invented as early as 1890 and though there were jukeboxes for seventy-eights, the first one for forty-fives was unveiled by the Seeburg Corporation around the same time as the very first single was released. Following their lead came the beautiful Art Deco-influenced masterpieces of pop design from Wurlitzer and Rockola.

Rather marvellously, these familiar trademarks are the actual names of the men who founded the companies: David Rockola and German immigrant Franz Rudolph Wurlitzer. There are plenty of examples of this, where someone's name has passed into common usage. I guess people know what you are referring to if you talk about your Dyson at a cocktail party, though they may well be looking over your shoulder to see if anyone more interesting is hoving into view. Hungarian László Bíró was the first to trademark the ballpoint pen and his fellow countryman Ernő Rubik came up with his annoying cube. The Dolby noise reduction system was the work of Ray Dolby from Portland, Oregon, and the saxophone was perfected in the 1840s by Belgium's Adolphe Sax. And unlikely though it seems, the high-end hi-fi company Bang & Olufsen was founded in Denmark in 1927 by Pete Bang and Svend Olufsen. Or have I made that one up? And can you be bothered to check?

Anyway, back to RCA Victor's green vinyl Country records. The first one issued, as we established earlier, was 'Texarkana Baby' by Eddy Arnold. He might not be mentioned much now, but he was a big name in the Fifties when his TV show took over Perry Como's slot. His songs spent a total of one hundred and forty-five weeks at number one on the US Country charts and sold over eighty-five million records. Signed to RCA, he was managed by Colonel Tom Parker, but would later find himself pushed down the roster when the 'Colonel' hooked up with some punk from Tupelo. Like Elvis, Eddy came from an impoverished background. Born in Henderson,

Tennessee, in 1918, his father was a sharecropper and eager for his son to earn a few dollars by working the land himself. Accordingly, despite having forged a musical reputation that took him to the Grand Ole Opry, his record was released under the billing of 'Eddy Arnold, The Tennessee PlowBoy and his guitar'. The record was released on 31 March 1949, making it the first single ever released if we ignore the demonstration record, which I think we have to. You can cop a listen to it online of course. It's pretty good, and though his guitar is certainly in evidence there are dandy bits of fiddle and lap steel too. It sounds a lot like Hank Williams, only cheerful. And as you listen to it now on whatever device you choose, imagine how thrilling it must have sounded on those early jukeboxes. Perhaps even a Seeburg with Wall-O-Matic tableside extensions.

So iconic and desirable have jukeboxes become that they are now targets for collectors and fetch huge amounts at auction. A Rockola 1414 President, a rather garish beast to my eyes, sold for one hundred and twenty-five thousand dollars, which sounds a lot, but you might be able to treat yourself to one if you find a gobbet of sperm whale spew on a beach somewhere.

12

The Time of Your Life

A lot of stuff happened in 1969. In January Richard Nixon was inaugurated as president of the USA, while that summer Neil Armstrong and Buzz Aldrin hopped out of the lunar module Eagle to become the first men on the moon – a matter of days after David Bowie released 'Space Oddity' on 11 July. Neil then uttered the immortal and oft quoted words: 'That's one small step for man, one giant leap for mankind.' Which actually makes no sense, as 'man' and 'mankind' mean the same thing in this context and there are those who suggest that he forgot to say 'a man' rather than just 'man', which would indeed sort out any syntactical problems. Armstrong has stated that he did say the missing 'a' but it was obscured by audio crackle. I've listened again and I don't think so. Sorry, Neil. In mitigation, I guess he had plenty of other stuff on his mind.

In other news, Concorde took to the skies for the first time, *Monty Python's Flying Circus* debuted on TV, the clans gathered for Woodstock in August and The Beatles played their last ever live performance on the roof of the headquarters of Apple Corps on Savile Row. Lennon was especially relieved to have fewer commitments as it left him plenty of time to mount his 'bed-in' for peace with Yoko Ono in the Presidential Suite of the Amsterdam Hilton, a happening they later restaged in Montreal. Less concerned with spreading a message of peace were the followers of Charles Manson who headed that fateful night to the house on Cielo Drive to brutally end the lives of Sharon Tate and her house guests.

Other people who were busy that year were Led Zeppelin, who unleashed their first two albums (and who would later perform their only duet with Sandy Denny on 'The Battle of Evermore'), and Jim Morrison of The Doors, who unleashed his penis from his leather trousers. This of course is not an offence in itself, but it apparently became so when enacted on stage at the Dinner Key Auditorium in Miami. I do love the music of The Doors but to fully appreciate them, I think, you have to be able to see past the fact that Jim was a bit of a pranny. At what point during a sellout gig, and presumably having ingested several chemical infusions, do you think: 'You know what this set needs right now? A glimpse of my flaccid todger.' And then, glancing down as your chipolata dangles rather pathetically, how quickly do you begin to realise that your judgement may have been flawed in this matter? I once had to introduce Iggy Pop on Channel 4's *The White Room* music show and he appeared wearing what looked like cellophane strides.

I think I heralded his performance with the words: 'He's here but will he get his knob out?' In truth this was a pretty much unnecessary query as he had shrinkwrapped his meat and two veg in the comfort of the dressing room before presenting them for all to behold.

However, in 1969 nobody could have been busier than Fairport Convention who went one better than even Zeppelin's achievements by releasing three albums. In a single year. Amazing, especially when you consider that one of them, *Liege & Lief*, is seen as a defining moment in folk rock and one of the most influential long players ever made. And also amazing, bearing in mind that in May of that year they suffered terrible losses when a road crash killed their drummer Martin Lamble and the girlfriend of lead guitarist Richard Thompson, Jeannie Franklyn.

Fairport Convention came together in a house called Fairport in Muswell Hill, which was also home to the medical practice of rhythm guitarist Simon Nicol's father. However the singer/songwriter who became a key force within the band in 1969, and who penned what listeners to BBC Radio 2 voted their favourite folk track of all time in 2007, wasn't there when the group formed. Alexandra Elene MacLean 'Sandy' Denny was born in 1947 in Merton Park, south London. Influenced and inspired by the traditional songs sung by her Scottish grandmother, she always had an interest in folk music, though she'd initially embarked on a nursing career. Giving that up, and gradually showing increasingly scant regard for matters of health, she undertook a foundation course at Kingston College of Art.

As early as 1966, though, she was being noticed as a singer, appearing on the BBC's *Folk-Song Cellar* radio programme. Her talents as a writer were also garnering attention and indeed by 1967, in the Summer of Love, she had recorded a demo of her most famous song, 'Who Knows Where the Time Goes?'. By some peculiar series of chance happenings, this tape was heard by Seattle-born folk superstar Judy Collins, who recorded it as a B-side to 'Both Sides Now'.

Now, clearly, under normal circumstances it would seem like insanity to have a song as utterly brilliant as 'Who Knows' as a B-side, were it not for the fact that an equally brilliant Joni Mitchell composition was on the A-side. In some ways, this release should have been a double A-side and would have been right up there in a 'best of' chart of records fitting into that category in which the undisputed number one would be The Beatles with 'Strawberry Fields Forever' and 'Penny Lane'. There have, however, been many incredible smash-hit songs that started life as humble B-sides. The Righteous Brothers' immortal classic 'Unchained Melody' of 1965 was initially on the 'other' side of the now forgotten 'Hung On You'. 'Behave Yourself' by Booker T. & The M.G.'s, anyone? No, me neither. Let's turn it over and see what's on the B-side. Hello, it's only 'Green Onions'. Even Rod Stewart's perennial favourite 'Maggie May' was launched as the flip side of the – admittedly pretty good – 'Reason to Believe'.

Amazing, too, to think that two solid gold rock and roll classics began this way. Elvis Presley's 'Don't Be

Cruel' is a great track but is it really better than the number on the other side, 'Hound Dog'? Perhaps even more extraordinarily, Bill Haley & His Comets released a single in 1954 entitled 'Thirteen Women (And Only One Man in Town'). This sounds less like a town and more like some deranged religious cult to me but, letting that go, any idea what was on the B-side? Yes. You're right. 'Rock Around the Clock'. And most amazingly of all, we know that Brian Wilson has often been prone to making unusual, some might say inadvisable, choices. Nevertheless there should have been someone who could have told him that fantastic though 'Wouldn't It Be Nice' was, the B-side 'God Only Knows', which Paul McCartney stated was the greatest record ever made, might be the real gem here. To be fair to Brian, the song was only released as a B-side in the States, out of concern that the title might offend religious sensibilities in the Bible Belt, despite seeming to confirm the omnipotence of the Almighty rather than detract from it.

Back to Sandy Denny, though, who joined Fairport Convention in 1968. She came in through auditions following the departure of original lead singer Judy Dyble. The group's annus mirabilis, if partially horribilis, of 1969 began with the release of *What We Did on Our Holidays*, which came out in January. One of Denny's major influences on the band, apart from diluting their self-confessed middle-class restraint with a healthy dose of free-spiritedness, was to urge them towards digging into the folk canon, which explains the presence here of the traditional songs, 'She Moves Through the Fair' and 'Nottamun Town'. There are also significant original compositions, like Richard Thompson's 'Meet on the Ledge' and Sandy's own 'Fotheringay', the latter of which would provide the name for her short-lived post-Fairport band.

At the very end of the year, being released in December, came the landmark *Liege & Lief*, generally accepted to be the most influential folk rock album ever. That is of course assuming that you accept it is a folk album – and there are those who don't. Certainly, when the band attempted to regroup after the tragic road accident, they found they were met with a certain resistance from folk traditionalists at their electric interpretations of some of the traditional standards. However, the band were adamant that these songs existed to be sung and played in different ways and not to lie in metaphorical glass cases in some imagined museum to be studied and not performed and enjoyed.

Three years after Bob Dylan was accused of being Judas for daring to plug in an electric guitar at Manchester's Free Trade Hall in 1966, *Liege & Lief* was, in a way, an experiment, a crusade to see if the folk tradition could be reclaimed and reinvigorated by the rockers. After all, Fairport had set out wanting to be an English version of The Byrds and initially had only a casual interest in folk music. Their eponymous debut album of 1968 includes no traditional songs at all. Perhaps then it's no surprise that when they spent those months in Farley House, rented for them by producer

Joe Boyd's office, in the Hampshire village of Farley Chamberlayne, getting the material together, the band considered themselves to be working on a side project.

The Fairport version of Sandy's masterpiece, 'Who Knows Where the Time Goes?', came out in July 1969 on *Unhalfbricking*, their second of three albums that year. The cover featured a photograph of a middle-aged couple standing in front of a suburban garden in which we catch a glimpse of the band through the fence. In the background is St Mary's Church, Wimbledon, for this is the Denny family home, and the man and woman in the foreground are Sandy's parents, Neil and Edna. The unusual title of the album evidently comes from a game called 'Ghost' played by the band on their interminable road trips to and from gigs. My understanding of it is limited, indeed negligible, but it seems to involve adding syllables without making a completed legitimate dictionary word.

Bands, of course, have many ways of trying to alleviate the endless tedium of those road miles. Clint Boon of Inspiral Carpets told me that in their early days they played hide-and-seek in a Ford Transit minibus. Once they progressed to the full-on sleeper coach with bunks, they devised 'Corridor of Death'. This involved everyone climbing into their bunks and kicking and punching wildly into the aisle while the victim ran down the full length of the vehicle, hopefully avoiding any meaningful contact save for the regulation winding and occasional black eye.

One of my favourite travel games is snappily titled 'Character Actors of the 1930s and '40s'. This entails looking for road signs which have the names of two or three locations emblazoned on them and which cumulatively look like the names of old thespians who worked regularly but never quite made it to stardom. This all began while visiting my in-laws and driving along the A49 towards Newbury. Along that charmless stretch of road I saw a sign that stated the next left would take me to Beedon and Chieveley. The 'and' is of course absent from the sign and so I like to think that Beedon Chieveley was a louche luvvie who played Lord Fancourt Babberley in *Charley's Aunt* at the Theatre Royal, Bury St Edmunds, in 1935. Indeed, Farley Chamberlayne – where *Unhalfbricking* was recorded – may also have been in the cast taking on the role of Colonel Sir Francis Chesney.

Sandy Denny lived a life of recklessness. She did indeed inject some wild-child abandon into the buttoned-down reserve of a band who were so hellbent on compromise they might easily have been rechristened Fair Point Convention. In some ways Sandy seems like a British counterpart of her contemporary Janis Joplin. Both were strong-willed women in a male-dominated world. Both had a bohemian and unfussy approach to style. Both were incredible singers, albeit with wildly differing styles as necessitated by the kinds of music they were drawn to. And both were unpredictable personalities. Joplin famously joined the '27 Club' in 1970, but Sandy wasn't far behind, checking out in 1978 at the age of just thirty-one. An habitual user of both drink and drugs, she exhibited classic manic-depressive symptoms which one suspects would be dealt with more sympathetically today.

Not even giving birth changed Sandy's behaviour. Her daughter Georgia was born prematurely in 1977 but Sandy seemed to have an erratic relationship with motherhood. Undoubtedly there were times of deeply sincere, if overbearing, care. Friends recall frantic phone calls in the middle of the night at some imagined ailment afflicting her daughter. And yet at other times she was said to be so drunk she would leave the infant in the pub. Certainly, her attention to her own wellbeing was negligible, although this may have been driven to some extent by what the broadcaster Bob Harris – who shared a house with her in Parsons Green, London, in 1968 – called her 'underlying melancholy'. Bob considered this to be driven, to some extent, by her difficulties in dealing with her rapid rise to fame but, whatever the reason, her drinking became self-destructive and she evidently fell off bar stools and down flights of stairs fairly regularly. Some called this 'Sandy's party trick' and, perhaps cruelly, branded it a deliberate attempt to get attention.

Certainly, she fell on a family holiday in Cornwall in March 1978 and then again at home in Northamptonshire. Concerned by her lifestyle, and taking a decision which understandably traumatised Sandy, her husband and musical partner in Fotheringay, Trevor Lucas, took their daughter Georgia back to his native Australia, selling the family car to raise the money for the air fares. He would later return to the Atkinson Morley Hospital in Wimbledon, and had to take the agonising decision of turning off

Sandy's life support machine as she lay in a brain-dead coma. She had suffered yet another fall, having been found at the bottom of the stairs in the home of friend Miranda Ward. Evidently there'd been one binge too many.

Sandy will be remembered for many great performances, compositions and interpretations but 'Who Knows Where the Time Goes?' will forever be her epitaph.

Even though it was voted the best folk song of all time, can it really be said to be folk? Our normal understanding of folk music is that it is the voice of the working classes and Fairport were resolutely middle-class. Folk songs are generally about specific incidents or ways of working or the natural landscape or expressions of inequality, and this song deals with none of those things. Does a folk song have to have existed for a century or more and be handed down orally across the generations? Shirley Collins and others think so, but I can't say I agree. Ralph McTell's 'Streets of London' is surely a folk song, with its prescient observations of the homeless, and though it only dates from 1968 it will be sung for certain in a hundred years' time – but it was a proper folk song the day it was written.

As, to my mind, was Sandy's song. It is about a feeling we have all experienced. That as we get older, time that seemed unlimited when we were younger, starts to slip by at an alarming rate. Quite beautifully this feeling is linked to the migration of birds, giving a folk connection to nature, and lending the track an exquisitely autumnal feel. In the way it is played and sung it is definitely music in the folk idiom and somehow there is a universality to it that seems to transcend genre. It has certainly come to be regarded as a classic by many folkies and so its acceptance would seem to suggest that a folk song can be newly written and crafted. Every song, no matter how old, has to be started by someone at some point, and if we want folk music to be a living, breathing entity then surely new material has to be accepted or we just become curators of antique collections.

Sandy was steeped in folk music and folk clubs and she utterly respected that grounding: it percolated through her and into the wonderful songs she wrote. In any case I think she expresses thoughts we have all had. When I was at Manchester University I had no concept of time, except for when the pubs shut as the archaic licensing laws waited for long overdue repeal, because three years was laid out before me and that seemed like an eternity. It was one-sixth of the life I'd had at that point and so it stretched out for ever. It didn't reach the horizon because the horizon had yet to come into view. There was no end in sight. And as I look back on that period of my life, I recall vividly how many memorable things happened and how many cast-iron friendships were forged. So many that it seems like it must have been ten years or more. However, it was all compressed into a mere three exhilarating years which somehow seems like a blip to me now.

Sadly, that classic line-up of Fairport Convention only lasted a blip of their own. They had broken up by the time *Liege & Lief* came out at the end of 1969. By the time of its release founder bassist Ashley Hutchings had left to throw himself fully into the folk scene, while Sandy Denny, having come from the folk clubs, had moved on to Fotheringay to showcase her own writing.

Of course, nothing lasts for ever and Sandy's end came much too soon. Whether in her quieter moments she felt that she wasn't going to be around for long, who can say? Her last public appearance was at a charity concert in her adopted home village of Byfield, Northamptonshire, where she spent the last four years of her life. And the last song she played? You know, in some ways given her humour and sense of mischief, I'd like to be able to write that it was something unexpected like George Formby's 'With My Little Stick of Blackpool Rock' or an acoustic version of the Sex Pistols' 'Anarchy in the UK'. It wasn't, though. It was 'Who Knows Where the Time Goes?'. Perhaps she knew the answer to that question, after all.

13

Culture Clash

A turning point for British culture and society undoubtedly occurred when the *Empire Windrush* docked in 1948 and deposited hundreds of British Caribbean people on these shores to face uncertain futures, as recent news coverage has dramatically revealed. A musical crossroads was also reached as immigration meant that it was inevitable that styles and influences from other nations would start to infiltrate white radio and the charts. Before the first wave of West Indians arrived, what might loosely be described as ethnic or world music, which was originally a term invented to describe music of the developing world, was more or less unknown in the UK. But the impact of the Windrush Generation's founders stepping ashore was felt immediately as newsreel footage was shot of the dapper, fedora-betopped, self-styled 'calypso king' Lord Kitchener singing 'London is the Place for Me'.

As more immigrants followed from the West Indies

more musicians inevitably arrived, and it was therefore no real surprise to see the Trinidad All Steel Percussion Band appearing at the Festival of Britain in 1951, which as we saw in Chapter 4 pointed the way to a brave new British world. Not least, one of racial integration.

The calypso became popularised as a satirical and comic song format on British television, thanks to the performances of the distinctly pale Lance Percival. All this helped to give what we might loosely call reggae a foothold in the collective consciousness and so it was perhaps inevitable that it would be the first 'foreign' sound to win widespread acceptance.

But it was a close-run thing. The fledgling hippie movement and search for a higher state of consciousness looked towards the meditational and musical techniques of India. As early as the summer of 1965, The Yardbirds were experimenting with sitar and tabla on 'Heart Full of Soul'. The final version retained the tabla but eschewed the sitar in favour of Jeff Beck's guitar imitating those distinctive drones. 'See My Friends' by The Kinks followed a month later and was clearly influenced by a trip to the subcontinent. By December, our old chums The Beatles were getting in on the act with George Harrison's sitar on 'Norwegian Wood' from the *Rubber Soul* album. Harrison then went one better the following year, when Indian instruments and flavours dominated 'Love You To' on *Revolver*.

So 'raga rock' was making its voice heard. There was, however, very little music of authentic African origin in evidence, until a recording made by anthropologists in

148

1967 of the drummers of Burundi became a 1971 hit under the name of 'Burundi Black'. We should also make note of Nana Mouskouri who had been exporting the music of her native Greece since the late Fifties. Originally from Crete but brought up in Athens, she has released well over two hundred albums in more than a dozen languages including Welsh, Mandarin, Hebrew and Corsican. It is almost impossible to be accurate but there are those who maintain she has sold more than three hundred million records. And all this with only one functioning vocal cord. Is she then the 'Godmother of World Music'?

Despite these plucky challengers, however, reggae, or perhaps more accurately ska, scored the first crucial chart breakthrough in 1964 when Chris Blackwell of Island Records paired singer Millie Small with a song called 'My Boy Lollipop'. Written by Robert Spencer of New York doo-wop group The Cadillacs in 1956, it first became a hit for Barbie Gaye under the title 'My Girl Lollypop', but Millie's remake eight years later established the music of the West Indies in the British hit parade. It went to number two, and Desmond Dekker and the Aces scored the first reggae number one in the UK in the spring of 1969 with 'Israelites'.

The appeal of reggae and its various subdivisions of mento, ska, bluebeat, dancehall, rock steady and dub is twofold. To the Western ear it is very much the sound of sunshine. Rather like the harmonies of The Beach Boys, it will always conjure up carefree days in a warm climate, so the lilting vibe of reggae is like aural Vitamin

D. Like the Island Records logo we are instantly transported to a land of beaches and palm trees. For many listening in the depths of a European winter that was more than welcome.

However, there is a deeper connection between reggae and the British Isles. The genre has always been a forum where the voices of the oppressed can be heard and there was certainly plenty of need for those as the optimism felt by the Windrush immigrants started to evaporate, with consequences that are still being felt and dealt with today. In America it seemed to bear echoes from the songs of slavery that had emanated from the cottonfields of the South thirty years earlier. Around the same time as reggae was gaining traction in the UK, Bob Dylan had picked up where Woody Guthrie left off to become the world's foremost protest singer. But there were equally potent voices – and to many a good deal more listenable – emerging from the reggae community.

As the Seventies began, the politicised teachings of Rastafarianism began to be a central thrust of the reggae movement. The doctrine centred on Haile Selassie, Emperor of Ethiopia between 1930 and 1974, who was seen as an earthly representative of the God we find within or 'Jah'. The songs of Rastafari called out to the African diaspora, who were marginalised by Western society, and urged them to return to the promised land of Zion in Africa where everyone would be equal. So reggae is in some ways folk music giving voice to the poor and disenfranchised. It campaigns for freedom from oppression and slavery. It is rejecting the imposed culture of the elite and so it is easy to see why it became such an easy bedfellow with the punk movement that emerged in the mid-Seventies. In some ways it's harder to use any of this to explain the affiliation between ska and the skinhead movement. Yes, both were emphatically working-class phenomena, but it seems unlikely that this connection alone was what brought the two together. It's not impossible though to think that there was a kinship in their shared outsider status. Reggae, with reverberations some maintain were inspired by the daily ricocheting gunfire in downtown Kingston, was the music of the ghetto. The skinheads, too, knew the tough side of life and considered themselves estranged from polite society, and so latched on to music that only rarely troubled mainstream media.

With the door prised open to the sound of reggae, the world was clearly ready for the first superstar to emerge from the scene – someone whose very presence would signify that, artistically, we were now living in a global village. This, in a sense, created another major moment in the history of pop. People began to accept that popular music was something that could come from anywhere in the world and not just Britain or the USA. Certainly Chris Blackwell understood this, and living in Jamaica he was infused with the culture while having a record label used to promoting rock acts back in London. It's actually pretty hard to overstate Blackwell's role here, as he was almost uniquely well placed to select the nascent star from the available talent pool and had the business brains and infrastructure to back his judgement.

He wanted an artist whose authenticity would be recognised by the captive audience, but would also be attractive to the general pop community.

Bob Marley was the perfect embodiment of these qualities, having established a musical credibility and also being an extremely good-looking man. He was an easy poster boy for the reggae genre. He had an air of mystery, of insouciance about him and yet it was all underpinned with a deeply felt connection to issues of inequality and oppression. He would later become an ardent advocate of Rastafarianism which would cement his place in the hearts of many of his countrymen. He would become as much a prophet and spokesman, indeed a folk hero, for his people as Dylan was to his.

Marley started out in the early Sixties recording with his key associates Bunny Wailer and Peter Tosh as The Teenagers. As a band name this is clearly short-sighted. Young and prodigiously talented they may well have been, but unless they thought they were going to have a very short career, the moniker wouldn't have been appropriate for long. Bob Marley was already eighteen by the time they started recording and so had only two teenage years left. Admittedly, Bunny was a couple of years younger but Tosh was a year older than Marley, giving him even less time before entering his twenties.

Funnily enough, I've discussed this point with another highly successful vocal trio, called The Young'uns. Sean Cooney, David Eagle and Michael Hughes hail from the northeast of England and took their name from the apprenticeship they served at Stockton folk club, where it's possible they might still be the young ones. They have grown into one of the most beloved acts on the folk circuit, combining incredibly precise close harmony with poignant songwriting and infectious good humour. However, their success has given them a career which will last way beyond even the loosest application of the word 'young'. Ultimately, when they are grey-haired and doddery, this will be a delicious irony, which they will make comic gold out of, but as they are yet to embark on middle age, it gives them an interesting challenge.

New Jersey pop band The Young Rascals, who had a monster hit in 1966 with 'Groovin'', eventually negotiated this issue by dropping the first part of their name and becoming simply The Rascals. The 'uns really isn't going to work in the same way, though, is it, lads? Similarly, Young Fathers can't really transmogrify into Fathers, it just doesn't sound right, but Young Grandfathers has a snappy ring to it assuming the fecundity of their various progeny.

Many pop and rock acts have found themselves in a similar predicament. The Heavy Metal Kids were fronted by vocalist and actor Gary Holton, who famously portrayed Wayne in *Auf Wiedersehen, Pet*. I actually saw Gary and his cohorts strutting their stuff at the Manchester Hard Rock supporting Uriah Heep in 1973, though I can't say I remember much about them; I was star-struck, having fallen into excitable conversation, on my part, with Heep drummer Lee Kerslake. I did ask him what he thought of Holton's crew and he deemed them to be 'alright, yeah'. Praise indeed. Clearly even by then the band didn't seem like kids. I was fifteen years old and Gary Holton was five years older than me, and so though their name had been plucked from the uber-cool works of William Burroughs, they still looked like aged geezers to me. Sadly, Holton wouldn't live to see old age, succumbing to the rock and roll lifestyle at the age of thirty-three. Amazingly, there does seem to be some current activity for the band even though any original member will be able to get to gigs with the aid of a senior railcard – as would I, were I to decide to go and see them. However, their raison d'être seems to be very much to pay tribute to their late lead singer and so I guess we can let them off treading the boards as 'kids'.

Boyzone and the Backstreet Boys would seem to have a similar problem, though, bizarrely, grown men have been referred to as boys even when the word gets beyond ridiculous. Morecambe and Wise were routinely dubbed 'the boys' right through to the end of their career. Girls Aloud would appear to have broken up before they had to consider becoming Women Aloud though of course the Spice Girls, or four of them anyway, have announced stadium shows as I write this.

The Small Faces neatly sidestepped any weight gain issues by simply becoming The Faces in late 1969, although it was a different band in many ways, involving a new singer and guitarist in Rod Stewart and Ronnie Wood, neither of whom is very big incidentally. The Small Faces were so named because they were well-known figures, or 'faces', on the Mod scene and were positively Lilliputian by today's free-range orange juice

Brobdingnagian proportions. Bassist Ronnie Lane and organist Ian McLagan were the twin colossi of the band at five feet and five inches; drummer Kenney Jones and frontman Steve Marriott came in an inch under that. Clearly, they were never going to get taller but had they survived long enough – and, sadly, only Kenney Jones remains – they might have easily succumbed to middle-aged spread or OAP obesity, which wouldn't have done at all. You could barely expect people to take you seriously as the Small Faces if you've eaten all the pies and developed numerous extra chins, short of stature though you have steadfastly remained.

Being fat in rock and roll or pop is a look that very few people have managed to pull off. If you do have a propensity to pile on the pounds, you're probably best advised to start out that way and make no secret of it. Like Meatloaf, for example, who even named himself after a kind of pie. Similarly Fats Waller, Fats Domino, The Fat Boys, Chubby Checker and the first person to record 'Hound Dog' – Big Mama Thornton – all used their not-inconsiderable girth as a trademark. If any of them had become Weight Watchers Slimmer of the Year, you suspect it would have been career suicide. Let's hope the Johannesburg-born, Doncaster-raised singer, song-writer, MC and all-round clever-trousers Skinny Pelembe doesn't start to overdo it at the all-day buffet. Essentially, if you are starting out on a pop career, it's worth getting a name that's going to last you – even though there are many examples of bands becoming very successful despite the name and I'm thinking very much of the inexplicably popular Kiss here. I mean no one in their right mind would want to snog them, would they? But being one smart cookie, Bob Marley quickly realised the limitations of his first group's name and The Teenagers became The Wailers before it was too late.

However, if Robert Nesta Marley became the first person to epitomise world music, it is ironic that a white man other than Chris Blackwell played a significant role in his breakthrough. Returning to recording in 1974, after a period wasted on heroin addiction, Eric Clapton – who in a further irony would later profess support for Rivers of Blood provocateur Enoch Powell (in a drunken onstage rant that inspired the Rock Against Racism movement) – took up residence to record an album at a rented house at 461 Ocean Boulevard in Golden Beach close to Miami. Seeking to make a new start, he basically worked on material that dismantled the idea of Clapton the guitar hero and one of the songs he chose was 'I Shot the Sheriff'. The song first appeared on one of the Wailers' true classic albums, 1973's *Burnin'*, and Marley's first to make even the gentlest ripple on the UK charts, reaching number sixty-seven, though failing to trouble the US charts at all. The Clapton version was released the following year and fared a little better – getting to number nine in Britain, and remaining his only American chart topper. Naturally Marley and Blackwell must have been glad of the attention that came their way in the aftermath of Eric's success, and though it would take a little while to travel, rebel rocker Bob's road to stardom opened up in front of him.

In a sense we reach three crossroads in quick succession here. The arrival of migrants from other shores began to alter the very fabric of our society. That led to many significant cultural shifts that shaped the world we lived in, not least in the way it modified our knowledge, understanding and acceptance of other musical idioms from around the globe. Those developments were life-changing for many people, but not least for Bob Marley, who would become the greatest world music star the world has ever known before dying at the age of thirty-six in 1981 of skin cancer. And the place of his death? Miami – where Clapton had first worked up the version of 'I Shot the Sheriff' that helped Marley on his way.

14

Ride That Train

And so, at roughly halfway on our, hopefully not too laborious, journey through this book, we reach a truly significant crossroads, where American and British influences intersected to create a short-lived scene, from which sprang the beat boom, the blues explosion and the folk revival. Its name was skiffle and it swept the UK throughout the mid-Fifties. At one point, there were thought to be between thirty and fifty thousand skiffle groups operating in the UK (though it's unclear how this figure was arrived at unless you had to disclose member-ship on your census form), including one on Merseyside called The Quarrymen.

When first confronted with those statistics I was dubious, but on further research, on the basis that there are approximately two thousand towns and, at the time of writing, sixty-nine cities in the UK, if you divide fifty thousand by two thousand and sixty-nine you come out with just over twenty-four. That still sounds like quite a lot, but as every town would play host to lots of dances with live music in church halls and the like, and there could well be hundreds of combos in London alone, the numbers look like they stack up. If you take the lower end of the estimate, i.e. thirty thousand, then each conurbation would have around fourteen bands. Then, if you subtract the number you first thought of, you will have worked out that Colin has seven apples left.

Okay, so enough of the maths, and anyway, thirty to fifty thousand? What kind of margin of error is twenty thousand? What kind of survey was that? Idiots. It's like a lot of research into radio audiences that even now is done by asking people to fill in listening diaries. I know. In these days of multiplatform downloadable Bluetooth online catch-up listen-again podcast app thought-pellet radio, we are still asking shadowy figures to scrawl in a pamphlet. Who are these mysterious phantoms? In my forty years of radio I can give you a much more accurate figure of how many of them I have met than the skiffle survey managed because it is none. It's actually frightening that careers can be decided on this most inexact of sciences and very frustrating, because if proper technological information gathering were involved I'm confident that the results would show that I am dead dead popular and great.

Skiffle music begins, like so much of the music we've looked at, in the American South. In the Twenties there was a popular phenomenon known as jug bands. These were groups formed by impoverished labourers who used household objects to make up for the lack of funds which prevented them from buying any musical instruments. True, you needed a guitar, and preferably a banjo, but the rhythm section could often consist of washboard and washtub bass with comb-and-paper kazoos also prevalent. The jug in question was a large glass bottle, into which low-end guttural sounds could be given extra resonance to sound like a tuba or sousaphone.

Extraordinary that a whole generation of bands should have been christened after a drunken buffoon belching into a demijohn, but such is the crazy world of rock and roll, kids. The jug band sound was largely consigned to history – as no one wanted to see an old soak expectorating into a massive jam jar – but it is worth noting that there were several bands who started out in this style and went on to have a major impact. The most notable was perhaps The Mugwumps whose members included Denny Doherty and Cass Elliot – both later of The Mamas and the Papas – as well as The Lovin' Spoonful's Zal Yanovsky and John Sebastian, the latter of whom penned a song called 'Jug Band Music'.

The sound also made an unlikely appearance at the top of the charts in 1970 when Mungo Jerry's 'In the Summertime' became a number one in Britain, Europe and Australia, and even climbed to number three on the *Billboard* charts in America. It is rumoured to have sold over thirty million copies – not bad for something that lead singer Ray Dorset said he wrote in ten minutes during a break at his day job of repairing Timex watches. We should therefore be able to trust his timekeeping. That means that for every sixty seconds he spent on the song, at least three million people bought it, which proves absolutely nothing but is pleasing nonetheless.

The first skiffle discs emerged in the early Twenties. Ma Rainey, born Gertrude Pridgett in Georgia and later christened 'The Mother of the Blues', made her first recordings in 1923 and reportedly told her audiences that her material was 'skiffle'. By 1925 'The Father of the Blues', aka Alabama-born W.C. Handy, and New Orleans pianist and legendary arranger Jelly Roll Morton were playing in a band called Jimmy O'Bryant and His Chicago Skifflers. The first appearance of the word 'skiffle' on a record came in 1929, when Don Burley and His Skiffle Boys released 'Hometown Skiffle', leaving you in very little doubt that skiffle was their game. Skiffle-mad, they were.

So why did this music undergo such a fervent revival in the UK in the Fifties? One of the reasons was that its lively, frenzied pulsating beat coincided with, and perhaps even paved the way for, rock and roll. It was thrilling for a younger generation, who were hooked on trad jazz but hadn't really experienced music specifically for teenagers. The other reason is that it was accessible to all. Unlike jazz you didn't need expensive instruments or highly developed musicianship. If you wanted to have a go, you just got up and did it. And that's punk rock right there: it was the birth of the DIY approach to music. The washtub bass of the jug bands was replaced by the more readily available tea chest and broom handle, but the washboards, kazoos and cheap guitars remained. If you wanted a band, you could have one. You didn't need years of music lessons – though someone was going to have to know a few basic chords – and you didn't have to save for your whole childhood to buy a drum kit. You and your mates could be a skiffle group over-night just like twenty-three other sets of pals in your home town. Or possibly thirteen sets of pals.

Lonnie Donegan, the figurehead of the British skiffle boom, was born Anthony James Donegan in Glasgow in 1931, to an Irish mother, and a Scottish father who played violin in the Scottish National Orchestra. The family moved to East Ham in 1933 and Anthony bought his first guitar in 1945, meaning he was set fair at exactly the right time and place to get involved with the skiffle scene at first hand. Changing his name to Lonnie after the New Orleans jazz guitar and fiddle player Lonnie Johnson, the first man to play an electrified violin, the young Donegan began to frequent the clubs and coffee bars of Soho and the West End of London, where the movement was quickly gathering pace. The first skiffle act to make any impact were the Bill Bailey Skiffle Group, who were operating as early as 1945, and it's easy to see how that untutored, energetic, raucous sound chimed with postwar euphoria. Even staid old Auntie, the BBC, realised something was going on and launched the *Saturday Skiffle Club* on national radio in 1957.

The key moment for Lonnie, though, came in 1953 with an audition for a jazz band led by a trumpeter from Great Yarmouth called Ken Colyer. His Jazzmen included clarinetist Monty Sunshine and the great trombonist and bass player Chris Barber, who would soon become a bandleader in his own right. Donegan managed to get an audition on banjo for Colyer's band, despite putting himself at what you'd have thought a crucial disadvantage by not owning one. However, he bought one on the way to that first meeting and evidently must have been a natural because he got the job. At that point he became something of a 'made man' on the London scene, since Colyer and Barber were not only top-notch players but very well connected in clubland. Not that recognised music venues were the lifeblood of skiffle.

One of the key ingredients of any musical revolution, be it, for example, skiffle, punk or acid house, is the co-opting of all kinds of spaces to be transformed into makeshift venues, and therefore having the ability to exist outside of the control of the mainstream promoters in the music business. Down the years scout huts, cellars, air-raid shelters, back rooms of pubs and fields in the middle of nowhere have all found themselves pressed into service as temporary gig spaces. With skiffle, the key locations were actually coffee bars – the most signif-icant being the 2i's on London's Old Compton Street.

It might seem odd that the pubs didn't play more of a part in this particular movement, but you have to remember that many fans of skiffle were teenagers and therefore unable to get into public houses. Also, the pubs – and clearly this is a sweeping generalisation – were fairly spartan places, with lino flooring, serving the flat-draught unpleasantness known as Watney's Red Barrel. The range of drinks would also include spirits and possibly Babycham, but wine and food would be conspicuous by their absence.

As would children. And music. So for the most part, boozers would consist of a snug bar populated by men in belted gabardine mackintoshes and flat caps supping pints of mild, and a lounge room where elaborately coiffured women in seersucker sipped Cherry B in the company of men in sports jackets supping halves of mild. By comparison the coffee bars with their hissing and crackling frothy cappuccino machines and thumping jukeboxes had a whiff of sophistication, of Continental glamour and of possibility. You were more likely to meet someone with ideas there. And you could get a cheese roll if you dropped by in your lunch hour.

The 2i's Coffee Bar got its name from Freddy and Sammy Irani who ran it until 1955, at which point it was taken over by two wrestlers – Ray Hunter and Paul Lincoln, whose nom de plume for the ring was Dr Death. Perhaps that would be enough to make you stop and think before arguing with the management. In fact, though there was no alcohol on sale, some security measures were evidently still seen as necessary. At nearby rival establishment, the Cat's Whisker on Kingsley Street, where future impresario Mickie Most worked as a waiter alongside Lionel Bart (the man who created the musical *Oliver!* and Tommy Steele's 'Rock with the Caveman', which was dubbed the first British rock and roll record), the bouncer was pugnacious man mountain Peter Grant, who would go on to terrorise promoters and ticket touts as manager of Led Zeppelin.

If you pay a visit to the Beatles Story exhibition at Liverpool's Albert Dock, you will pass through a facsimile of the legendary Cavern club. Admittedly, you can still go to the 'actual' Cavern, though it is for the most part a recreation of the hallowed original – partially on the same site and not without a certain atmosphere. But at Albert Dock, the first thing that will strike you is the size of the place. It's not uncommon these days to find people whose sitting rooms are bigger than the Cavern, although admittedly not many of them have a snack bar in the corner with a display case for the all-important cheese and ham rolls. The Cavern was indeed so unprepossessing that it didn't even have a poured concrete floor: you would instead have to make do with tapping your slingback or Chelsea boot on asphalt. The cellar of the 2i's did at least have the luxury of proper flooring – London, eh? Though that was, if anything, even smaller. The 'stage' at one end, was made of planks and beer crates and had a depth of about eighteen inches; yet it was here that Cliff Richard and Tommy Steele began to make names for themselves in front of audiences of twenty to thirty people. Presumably that cellar is still down there somewhere, and I'm told there is a fish and chip shop on the site of the premises. What a shame that the place that can perhaps make the strongest claim to being the birthplace of British rock and roll isn't available to visit now.

Lonne Donegan frequented the 2i's and the Soho circuit as his reputation began to grow and so it seemed inevitable he would think about making his own disc. He had begun to record with Ken Colyer's Jazzmen in 1953, but in 1954 headed into the studio to lay down the track that would change his life. Creating a thrift-store power trio with Chris Barber on bass and on washboard the musician and singer Beryl Bryden,* Donegan decided to have a crack at the Leadbelly standard, 'Rock Island Line'. This track, named for the railroad running from Chicago all the way to New Orleans, was first recorded in 1934 by inmates at Arkansas Cummins State Farm Prison. Leadbelly was not a prisoner, but hc is thought to have been there offering some guitar backing at that historic session and subsequently began performing the song until it became one of his signature numbers. With its building ferocity and unpolished charm, the Lonnie version finally became a UK top ten hit in 1956, charting for several months and firing up the imagination of the nation's youth. It even, in a coals-to-Newcastle kind of way, reached the top ten in the States too. It sold over a million copies and was the first UK debut record to go gold. Not a bad way to open your account.

The skiffle boom was largely over by 1958 but it didn't matter. The touch-paper had been lit. Lonnie Donegan began to make music hall-style novelty hits like 'Does Your Chewing Gum Lose Its Flavour on the Bedpost Overnight' (1959) and 'My Old Man's a Dustman' (1960) before becoming a fixture on the variety circuit for many years to come. He passed away in 2002, but his legacy was assured. How many people can genuinely say they

---

* Bryden has a remarkable story of her own and was once dubbed 'Britain's Queen of the Blues' by Ella Fitzgerald no less.

altered the course of British rock and roll, and popular music in general?

Just as The Velvet Underground inspired countless artists to form bands, despite none of their LPs hitting the charts on their initial release, the UK wave of skiffle – and Lonnie Donegan's 'Rock Island Line' in particular – led the charge in a similar way. Nobody had to wait to be given permission any more – a message not lost on Van Morrison, Alexis Korner, Alex Harvey, Ronnie Wood, Mick Jagger, Jimmy Page, Roger Daltrey, Ritchie Blackmore, David Gilmour, Johnny Kidd, Albert Lee, Graham Nash and Allan Clarke of The Hollies, and The Shadows. Even Barry Gibb had his own skiffle group called The Rattlesnakes. You can begin to see, just from that by no means exhaustive list, what an impact that couple of years in the basements of Soho had on subsequent waves of the British music scene.

Donegan's legacy was reconfirmed in 1978 when he rerecorded many of his early songs with musicians including Rory Gallagher, Brian May, Ringo Starr and Elton John – which is a pretty good backing band by anyone's standards. So indebted did Van Morrison feel that in 2000 he released an album called *The Skiffle Sessions – Live in Belfast* for which he shared the stage with Lonnie and Chris Barber. Meanwhile, for his 2004 solo album, *Shangri-La*, Mark Knopfler wrote a song in tribute titled 'Donegan's Gone'.

In 2019, while flicking through TV channels, I happened upon an audition on ITV's *The Voice* by one of Lonnie Donegan's sons, Peter, who performed playing his father's guitar. In a very special moment he fell into conversation with Sir Tom Jones. Their chat led, seemingly spontaneously, into an impromptu duet on a song called 'I'll Never Fall in Love Again', which Lonnie had co-written, and which Tom had recorded, in the Sixties. Their duet had a poignancy you don't witness very often on telly, and it made me glad that the name and reputation of someone who shaped the music we take for granted remains in circulation. Truly, Lonnie Donegan gave thousands of people who wanted to be in a band – or thought they had something to say in a song but hadn't had proper musical training – the guts to do it. He understood this was a big part of what 'music for the people' meant, and as he said himself:

> 'I'm trying to sing acceptable folk music but I want to widen the audience beyond the artsy-crafty crowd and the pseudo intellectuals but without distorting the music itself.'

Amen to that, Lonnie. Amen to that.

15

From the Laboratory to the Dancefloor

In 1989 a genre-defining romcom hit the screens. Directed by Rob Reiner – who had already secured a place in our hearts for ever by masterminding *This is Spinal Tap* in 1984, *When Harry Met Sally . . .* was the story of Sally Albright, played by Meg Ryan, and her tortuous 'will they, won't they' friendship with Billy Crystal's Harry Burns.

A sweet element of *When Harry Met Sally . . .* is the intercut sequences, where fictitious couples tell us how they first met. Of course, the main thing anyone remembers about the movie is the fake orgasm scene. Sally performs this to prove to Harry that a bloke can't tell when a woman is faking it: although if she is sitting at a table in a New York diner an educated guess would always be 'faking'. In fact, so celebrated has this part of the film become that, at that table in Katz's Delicatessen, Manhattan, a sign hangs stating: 'Where Harry met Sally. Hope you have what she had. Enjoy.' This refers to the oft-quoted closing lines of the scene, where an older woman* witnesses Meg's orgasmic ecstasies. The director has often commented that in previews, when viewing this encounter, women became hysterical with laughter while men generally squirmed in embarrassment. Perhaps since then the audible, female faked orgasm has become something much more commonplace in popular culture with the ubiquity of the internet, but back then, for many males, it could well have been the first time they'd heard anything like it.

The first time I heard anything like it came in 1975 – and don't worry, we are not getting into braggadocious tales of the youthful Radcliffe libido here, and even if we were it would scarcely have resulted in the kind of vocal outpourings we've been describing. A more likely sound in those few and far between scenarios would have been the hysterical laughter at Rob Reiner's previews.

Anyhow, in the mid-Seventies, while studying for my A Levels at Bolton School, I had a Saturday afternoon job at the *Bolton Evening News*. This involved sitting in a room with several other adolescents, both male and female, and donning a telephone headset to write down reports of local cricket or football matches that were being phoned in by cub reporters. While we waited for half- or full-time, or innings updates, we would have pop music playing on the radio and one of the records that came up quite a lot was 'Love to Love You Baby'

---

* Portrayed by Rob Reiner's mother.

by Donna Summer. This basically consisted of a funky, Blackalicious disco beat over which, at some length, Donna seemed to be emphatically having what Sally was having. However, Donna was not in a deli, which at least gave, ahem, rise to the possibility that she really was having it.

The sound of this record gave a tantalising glimpse into a world I hoped very much to visit one day, but also led to much nervous coughing and shuffling of papers in the newspaper office; it was something not particularly easy to take in one's youthful stride while in the presence of attractive girls of roughly the same age. It was notable that the assembled females didn't seem to be exactly rolling around in the aisles as they had done at the film showcase, either. I guess we were all just too immature and crippled with awkwardness with the opposite sex to deal with this in any sensible way, though when my fellow copy-taker Adrian Hewitt asked, 'Just what is that girl doing?', as Summer once again reached her rumpy-pumpy rapture, the looks of disdain were withering.

We later found out the 'girl' in question, unlikely as it sounds, shared a name with the sexually untested Master Hewitt, as she was christened LaDonna Adrian Gaines, born in Boston, Massachusetts in 1948. Donna Summer would come to be ranked *Billboard* magazine's sixth most successful dance act of all time and took an interesting path to get there. She started out as lead vocalist for psychedelic rockers Black Crow and also had a spell in the musical *Hair* before moving to

Germany, where she met the man who would transform her fortunes: Giorgio Moroder.

Moroder was born in that hotbed of disco, Italy's South Tyrol in 1940, but relocated to Munich where he set up the state-of-the-art recording complex Musicland Studios. Initially he planned to launch himself as a solo artist and indeed had some success as early as 1969 with a song called 'Looky Looky', which sounds rather like 'Papa Oom Mow Mow' by The Rivingtons. There is an absolutely hilarious, if vaguely terrifying, video clip of it on YouTube. Have a look and you will swear it is some spoof created by the great Matt Berry for *Toast of London* or something similar. That this Open University geology professor-alike would later be heralded as 'The Father of Disco' and the epitome of cool – going on to work with David Bowie, Cher, Kylie Minogue, Japan, Janet Jackson, Blondie and Irene Cara – is little short of incredible. And probably means he's all right for a few bob.

'Looky Looky' also sounds like a prototype for Moroder's later composition, 'Son of My Father', which he recorded and released under the name Giorgio in 1971. However, it became a number one hit in the UK in 1972 for Chicory Tip and is the first chart-topper to feature a synthesizer.

The first time I can remember a Moog synthesizer mentioned on the sleeve notes of a record was when it was credited to Ralph Mace on David Bowie's 1970 *The Man Who Sold the World* album, though it took a couple of years for it to progress to the high reaches of the charts, when Chicory Tip's football-terrace classic would be joined by Elton John's 'Rocket Man' with its prominent synth interjections. Intriguingly, in clips of Chicory Tip on *Top of the Pops*, their keyboard player is miming the part on an electric piano, demonstrating that the Moog was still a comparatively rare beast and certainly far too valuable to be lent out to a band of foot-stomping wallies who would probably leave it unattended while they tried to get off with Pan's People.

The Moog synthesizer was a formidable piece of equipment. A keyboard with associated patch bays and wires resembling a small telephone exchange, it looked like you would need to be a NASA scientist to operate it; many early pioneers talk of their frustration at chancing upon a wonderful sound from another galaxy, only to find there was absolutely no way of reconstituting the same settings. Part of the wonder of the thing was that it was unpredictable and took you into unchartered musical territory on a regular basis.

Robert Moog first displayed his magical machine in public at the Audio Engineering Society Convention in New York in 1964. There had been synthesizers prior to that, but they were cumbersome devices that filled whole rooms and Moog realised that portability was going to be key to any conceivable commercial success. His initial pricing point was around ten thousand dollars, however, and if you think that sounds like quite a lot you'd be right, considering that the average house price in the UK was around three thousand pounds. So clearly the Moog was only going to be attainable to the very

175

wealthy which makes it slightly less surprising then to learn that the first synth used on a record belonged to Micky Dolenz of The Monkees and was pressed into service on their 1967 American number one album *Pisces, Aquarius, Capricorn and Jones Ltd*. The Doors utilised one the same year on *Strange Days*, but perhaps the quantum leap publicity-wise came in 1968 when Walter Carlos released the seminal *Switched-On Bach*, which reworked Johann Sebastian's familiar repertoire of cantatas, concertos and fugues for the synth. For a project that must have seemed totally 'out there' at the time it was incredibly successful. It won several Grammy awards and was a fixture in the upper reaches of the *Billboard* classical charts continuously between 1969 and 1972, even reaching number ten on the general chart, and selling over a million copies. A happy consequence of the money it generated was that it allowed Carlos to have gender reassignment surgery and make the switch from Walter to Wendy.

Gradually, and particularly once the more affordable Minimoog had been introduced in 1970, the synth became something no self-respecting keyboard player would be without. Certainly, for the progressive rock fraternity it became little short of essential and there were acts whose music was generated almost entirely electronically, like Tangerine Dream and Tonto's Expanding Head Band. Japanese musician Tomita followed the trail forged by Walter Carlos, with his 1974 long player *Snowflakes Are Dancing*, which featured synthesized settings of Claude Debussy's tone poems.

Kraftwerk would eventually refine their output, which initially utilised wind and other instruments as well as their trademark electronics, to become perhaps the most iconic example of the electronic genre there has yet been.

After 'Love to Love You Baby', Moroder and Summer's other huge landmark record was 'I Feel Love', released in 1977. Another work of genius, it is, though less orgasmic than its predecessor, equally sensual yet driven by a pulsating electronic beat and rapid synth sequences. The genius of this track, and why it turned popular music on its axis so dramatically, was that it took electronica away from the rather academic and esoteric community and into the realms of sexy pop. When Kraftwerk released their classic tracks 'Showroom Dummies' and 'The Robots' in the late Seventies, they cemented the idea that this was music made by automata, paving the way for Gary Numan to ponder the all-important question as to whether 'friends' were electric. Eventually, though they were never sexy, it became clear that there was at least a more playful side to Kraftwerk, as they talked of their love of disco dancing and messing around with pocket calculators. And though 'Son of My Father' and 'Rocket Man' had demonstrated there was certainly room for the synth in fun pop, those records hadn't utilised electronic rhythms as the driving force or implied any human carnality. What Moroder did, though, on 'I Feel Love' was to harness the highly sexualised image of Donna Summer and unite it with a relentless artificially generated pulse.

Summer would later become a born-again Christian

and found being dubbed 'The First Lady of Love' somewhat embarrassing, but in the mid-Seventies she threw herself into it wholeheartedly. In 1974 she released an album called *Lady of the Night*, and though initially reluctant to go the whole Sally for 'Love to Love You Baby' a year later, certainly got there in the end. The first version of the track was single length and was sent by Giorgio to a record company boss in the States who found it went down exceedingly well at his debauched parties in the Hollywood hills. The only problem was that it wasn't long enough, leading to the celebrated twelve-inch version which ran to over sixteen minutes.

Apparently Summer could only lose sufficient inhibition to perform the extended version by imagining herself to be an actress like Marilyn Monroe (unfortunately Meg Ryan wasn't around for inspiration just yet), playing the part of someone experiencing ecstasy. Even then she insisted on recording it in complete darkness. However they did it, the end results were compelling and the final count, though I admit I haven't checked this myself, being unsure of my own judgement, is twenty-three orgasms in sixteen minutes. Which is pretty good going by anyone's standards. Isn't it?

After 'Love to Love You Baby' became a global hit in 1975, Moroder linked all the suggestiveness he and Donna had created and put it to a driving sequenced rhythm track for 'I Feel Love'. It proved that electronic music didn't have to be cold and robotic, but could be sexy too. Nowadays this concept seems so obvious. Listen to a track like Depeche Mode's 'Master and Servant' and though I'm not entirely sure what the games they're suggesting entail, I'm pretty sure they're quite a long way from Jeeves and Wooster. Even a track like Frankie Goes to Hollywood's 'Relax' – while not exclusively electronic – used the latest sampling and programming technology to carry a potent sexual message. The reliably prudish BBC famously banned that track but they had a proven track record in this respect, having banned 'Love to Love You Baby' too – which admittedly would have sounded somewhat out of place on the Jimmy Young programme.

In fact, electronic music would become increasingly sexualised, particularly in the hedonistic New York disco days before the AIDS epidemic took hold. Even as the epidemic kicked in, tracks like 'Do You Wanna Funk' by Patrick Cowley and Sylvester, Divine's 'Native Love' and 'Passion' by the Flirts as well as 1986's 'Male Stripper' by Man 2 Man Meets Man Parrish, positively throbbed with the promise of nights of PVC-clad abandon. Is it too much to suggest that as sexual habits grew increasingly liberal and experimental, and began to routinely involve battery-powered handheld devices, the union of electronic music and sex became a wholly natural thing?

Giorgio Moroder has had many musical achievements, not least the soundtrack to *Midnight Express*, and once stated that he thought his personal career high point was producing and co-writing 'Take My Breath Away' by Berlin. I'd have to disagree. He and

Donna Summer's work on 'I Feel Love' took electronic music out of the laboratory and not only onto the dancefloor but into the bedroom, too. Things would never be quite the same again.

16

Trouble in Motor City

A world away from the highly polished and sexualised disco records Giorgio Moroder so brilliantly constructed is the primal, snotty yelp of punk. An undoubted revolution, punk changed the face of popular music for a time and so its point of origin has to be a crucial intersection on our journey through pop. So where does punk rock begin, and what does the term even mean? There are those who maintain that year zero is 1976 and that the first true punk was Television's Richard Hell who was the initiator of wearing the safety pin as a fashion item and general badge of honour. But to my mind, it has to go back way before that. To be a true punk band, you need to be anti-establishment with some degree of political infusion, write your own short songs, be very noisy, play very fast, and preferably not for very long, break up after quite a short time as punks are supposed to be young, and cut your own hair short with a razor. So, who are the first band to tick all of those boxes?

Our first contenders came out of the American garage band tradition, i.e. bands rehearsing with guitars in garages and not to be confused with the UK garage scene of Craig David, Artful Dodger and So Solid Crew. The Sonics, from Tacoma, Washington, were up and running by 1960 and their debut album *Here Are the Sonics* was released in 1965. To give them their due, they do make a lot of the requisite noises and their hair certainly isn't long, but that LP is very cover-heavy and you can't really claim to be at the forefront of change if you are churning out yet more versions of 'Roll Over Beethoven', 'Money (That's What I Want)' and 'Good Golly Miss Molly'. Those songs had already been the sound of teen angst and restlessness and so couldn't be revolutionary a second or even third time around. You might ask why composing your own material is so vital to this argument but if punk means a do-it-yourself ethic then that has to extend to the writing. For starters, you ought to have something that you're bursting to say about the times you find yourself living in. And also, as most self-respecting punk bands employed a degree of at least some ineptitude, you ought only to be capable of playing your own songs: that way no one can tell you you're doing it wrong. In addition, if being punk means starting out on something new then you must, by definition, be playing new stuff and not just recycling the past, no matter how spunky you make it. So, the Sonics, I love you guys but you've just missed out here.

We then have to make a little leap to 1964, as it's a

well-known fact, that I've just conveniently made up, that no bands were formed between 1961 and 1963. Actually that's not a bad idea. Clearly, there are far too many bands so there should be some 'fallow' years in which it is against the law to form one.

In 1964, The Troggs were beginning to make a rumble in Andover and while they had a certain punkish direct-ness they still wanted to be pop stars. Around the same time, or maybe slightly earlier, The Animals in Newcastle upon Tyne were displaying the feral charms which gave them a certain undesirable edge. But the two bands who can most accurately be described as punk kick off in 1964 and they're both in America.

One of them is The Velvet Undergound, but there are some problems here. First, their hair is a bit longer than is ideal. In fact, Lou Reed often bears an uncanny resem-blance to Edmund Blackadder while John Cale has a well-topiarised page-boy cut with which Mary Quant would have been very pleased. Also, a lot of their songs are a bit mellow. Their 1967 debut record, *The Velvet Underground & Nico*, opens with the haunting and rather lovely 'Sunday Morning' and it's only by track two and 'Waiting for My Man' that we get some energy pulsing through the veins. Certainly, the Velvets influ-enced many musicians: they stood for creating art on their own terms, or at least the bits that Andy Warhol hadn't helped them with, and breaking away from the rules of what a pop group had to be. Also on the plus side, they were more than happy to make an almost unlistenable racket for minutes on end, which was certainly a rejection of the mainstream, especially as it involved the scraping of Cale's viola. But is a viola punk? Complicated, isn't it?

When I was a drummer in numerous bands during my schooldays, I was often paired in the rhythm section with a bass player called Mark 'Beefy' Byers. I should say in his defence that the 'beefy' epithet came about due to his throbbing sound and not because he had binged on pies and brown ale. Accordingly we spent a good deal of time together talking about what we'd do with our millions when we'd 'made it', and playing each other amazing records we'd heard. One day in his bedroom in Chorley, in the summer of 1975, he showed me a record by a band called MC5. The sleeve looked garish and thrilling somehow. Glossy photographs of the band, most notice-ably the gap-toothed lead singer Rob Tyner looking like some kind of deranged David Mellor, were superimposed over each other along with crowd shots and the American flag. Once we put the record on the Garrard turntable, we discovered that the band's performance was just as thrilling as the cover had led us to expect. The record opens with 'Ramblin' Rose': a blistering explosion of uncontrolled guitar-led rock and roll punctuated by the hysterical falsetto of Tyner. I don't recall having heard anything with that level of unbridled ferocity before. Beefy and I sat and looked at each other wide-eyed, and not just because of the mushrooms. It felt like the start of a revolution had been captured for posterity on vinyl.

And so, after much consideration, we can award the honour of first punk band to the MC5, not least because they come screaming out of Detroit a good four or five years before their near neighbours Iggy Pop and The Stooges. Let's examine their credentials.

As regards being anti-establishment and politically infused, these guys had it all going on. They were practically street fighters coming from some of the meanest neighbourhoods Detroit had to offer. Childhood friends and guitarists Wayne Kramer and Fred 'Sonic' Smith, who would later marry Patti Smith, had both formed bands (The Bounty Hunters and The Vibratones respectively), but decided to pool their talents. They were heavily influenced by the aggression and excitement they heard in garage and surf music, but knew they had to do something harder-edged. They were emphatically of the counterculture, yet when we think of that term we tend to have in mind stoned hippies with headbands and cheesecloth smocks dancing like fronds of seaweed in a drifting current. Instead, MC5 came from the frontline where poverty and social unrest were the sparks.

The mid-Sixties in America were incendiary times of change. Many of the inner cities were tinderboxes scarcely controlled by police forces who resorted to brutality to keep a lid on things, often inflaming already fragile situations until violence erupted on all sides. This was certainly true of Oakland, California, where, in 1966, out of more than six hundred officers only sixteen were black and so the Black Panther movement was duly born. Initially intended as a vigilante squad to combat the violence meted out by the cops, their activities eventually extended to helping the needy and aiding

185

community cohesion through schemes such as tuberculosis testing and distributing free breakfasts to impoverished schoolkids. There was an underpinning of egalitarian principle to everything the Black Panthers stood for. Every enrolled member was prescribed Mao's *Little Red Book* as essential reading and the struggle for economic equality was a central tenet.

The fact that the FBI's notoriously volatile and paranoid director J. Edgar Hoover described the Black Panthers as 'the greatest threat to the internal security of the country' shows just how widespread their influence had grown from its Californian roots. The plight of black people living in ghetto-like conditions, and discriminated against in every aspect of life, education and work was familiar to all first-generation descendants of those who'd migrated north. This was graphically true in Detroit where, although there was work for all in the car plants, rates of pay and standards of housing available to blacks were considerably lower than those for whites. Frustration and justifiable anger grew, eventually spilling out during the long hot summer of 1967 when the Detroit Rebellion, or 12th Street Riots, took place.

The initial flash point was the raiding of an unlicensed drinking club frequented by the black community. Things quickly got out of hand when the police decided to arrest everyone there and a large crowd gathered. In the aftermath of the troubles there were said to have been forty-three deaths (thirty-three black and ten white casualties), more than seven thousand arrests and two thousand buildings pretty much destroyed.

The Detriot riots of 1967 and their repercussions were events the members of MC5 – Kramer, Smith, Rob Tyner, Michael Davis and Dennis Thompson – were witnessing first-hand and so is it any surprise that their music turned out the way it did? Of course many white residents of Detroit would have made sure they never ventured into those unstable areas, but Kramer, Smith and co. felt that their own backgrounds gave them more of a connection and solidarity with the oppressed black communities than with the comparatively bourgeois whites. They felt it was a dereliction of duty to turn a blind eye to the conflict ravaging their city.

MC5 were also influenced by another organisation called Up Against the Wall Motherfucker, which grew out of the anti-Vietnam war movement in New York. This sect in turn was an offshoot of a group called Black Mask who sought to mix radical politics and art. Not only did they cut the fences at Woodstock to allow free access to thousands, they also managed to get inside the Pentagon. The social activist Abbie Hoffman called them 'the middle-class nightmare'. That the MC5 were majorly influenced by all of this was confirmed by the full uncensored title of their 1969 debut album's title track: 'Kick Out the Jams, Motherfuckers', which was routinely sanitised as 'Kick Out the Jams, Brothers and Sisters'. The 'full-fat' title would later lead to Detroit department store Hudson's refusing to stock the record and eventually, by association, all product on Elektra, the label on which it appeared. This would lead to a parting of the ways between the band and Elektra.

So, despite, or perhaps because of, all their anti-establishment leanings and pronouncements MC5 were a relatively hot property, drawing crowds of up to a thousand in their home city from the early days. In fact, on a 1968 tour of the East Coast of the US they were routinely upstaging the acts they were supporting including Big Brother and the Holding Company and, one imagines a somewhat chastened, Cream.

It's fair to say, then, in terms of political credibility and activism the MC5 have impeccable credentials. They also wrote their own material for the most part. The album *Kick Out the Jams* included the track 'Motor City is Burning', which had been performed by John Lee Hooker amongst others, but then again, as they were the Motor City 5, that can be forgiven, and they had also radicalised it by making mention of the snipers reportedly utilised by the Black Panthers in the 1967 insurrection. They also credited the legendary Alabaman jazz pianist, band leader and poet Sun Ra on the song 'Starship' which was, and is, an incredibly hip reference. Okay, punk may not have much to do with jazz musically, but it has plenty to do with free jazz in approach and the band were more than happy to acknowledge that they'd been influenced sonically by the squealing saxophones of the likes of John Coltrane and Albert Ayler. Further covers followed on their second album in 1970, not only Little Richard's 'Tutti Frutti' but also its title track, a reworking of Chuck Berry's 'Back in the USA', but as they were active in pursuing a very different kind of USA, again, I think they can be forgiven for this. For their third collection, *High Time*, every track was an MC5 original.

Their songs then were by and large their own, so what of their live shows? Were they the sort of short, sharp shocks we've deemed essential in punk? Yes. Their debut album was recorded across two nights at Detroit's Grande Ballroom on the 30 and 31 October 1968 as it was realised that to experience them live was to witness them at the height of their powers. First-hand spectators talk of them having such raw power that it seemed as if they could scarcely control it, and in the aftermath you would often feel that you'd witnessed a street fight. Playing gigs in a segregated society to black and white kids united at the fringes of society, one can only imagine how compelling a live proposition they were. They also kept it relatively short compared to the hippie bands of the day, except for one notable exception: while playing an anti-Vietnam concert during the 1968 Democratic National Convention, as other artists were prevented from appearing by a police-induced riot, the MC5 played for a Grateful Dead-like eight hours straight.

Okay, so far so good on the punk credentials. They were politically motivated, wrote their own songs and were incendiary live. To set their legacy in stone they just had to make sure they didn't hang around too long. Here again they score a bullseye. By 1972 it was all over. Whether this had anything to do with their commercial fortunes is unclear, but they certainly sold progressively fewer records as they went on. *Kick Out the Jams* reached number thirty in the American charts while *Back in the*

USA stalled at one hundred and thirty-seven with *High Time* faring even less well than that. But when you explode onto the scene the way they did it is almost impossible to sustain such an impact, and so being relatively short-lived made them more precious still.

And they are precious. You can make a strong case for Detroit having been the most important music city there has ever been. Thanks again to the Great Migration, its blues, gospel, soul and jazz roots are impeccable. It has produced the proto-punks and a major hardcore punk scene. Detroit techno became a global phenomenon as did the white boy hip hop of Eminem. It has given rise to many stars from Aretha Franklin, who moved to the city as a five-year-old, Diana Ross and Smokey Robinson to Madonna, Iggy Pop, Ted Nugent, Alice Cooper, Glenn Frey of The Eagles, Bob Seger, Aaliyah, Was (Not Was), Jack White – and unfortunately Kiss. But if we accept that the MC5 kicked off punk then their importance is pretty hard to overstate. It was fast, loud, brief, radical, and it stuck it to the man.

Sad then that they fell at the last hurdle. Tonsorially they were like the Hair Bear Bunch. Thompson, Davis and Smith had lank shoulder-length locks. Though elegantly bald now, Wayne Kramer had a lustrous topping of Syd Barrett-style curls and lead vocalist Rob Tyner sported a full-on Afro, perhaps to show solidarity with the Black Panther brothers. So there's the final conundrum. They were the band who invented punk but they didn't have punk hair.

17

The Voice of Protest

In 2015 I made a series for BBC Four called *Music for Misfits: The Story of Indie,* with the brilliant film-maker Matt O'Casey. During filming we set up a camera on Whitworth Street West in Manchester in order to get a shot of me, desperately trying to remember what I was supposed to be saying, with the Hacienda Apartments in the background marking the location of that celebrated and ultimately doomed nightclub.

As we started to roll, a burly fellow in suit trousers and a fleece asked if he could see our permit. We admitted that we did not have such a document as we were merely recording me spouting some stuff with the remains of the Hac behind me and anyway what did it have to do with him as we were on a public street? He was bigger than us, so we may have put it more cordially than that. He explained that, despite the fact that we were on a street where members of the public freely walked, we were in fact on private property. Therefore while simple perambulatory excursions were allowed, anything like filming had to be preapproved. He said that we would have to stop what we were doing while he went to refer the matter to his superior.

Bemused, we waited until an icily polite and pristine young woman with ironed hair and a regulation black jacket and skirt arrived to confirm that permission had to be applied for and given in writing in advance. I pointed out that we had no idea we were anywhere but on public land and that anyway, we weren't taking any shots of their private street, just putting a camera on it to record what was across the road. She calmly replied with the chilling statement that, unfortunately for us, the pavement we were standing on did fall within a private estate which they sought to monetise. It was the first time I had ever heard that word and it amazed me that we were being asked to pay to stand on a footpath in the city I love, which has been my home since 1976. She also made it clear that if we were prepared to pay (we weren't), we would have to go away and seek permission in writing before coming back with the requisite paperwork. So, if you watch that programme and think that the Hacienda Apartments rear up at a dizzying angle behind me you will understand that we had no option but to do the link across the road. What would Woody Guthrie have made of it? This land didn't feel like my land that day.

Maybe you haven't heard of Woody Guthrie, but without him there would have been no Bob Dylan, and although the idea of protest singing might have come along eventually Woody certainly got the ball rolling. He was an 'Okie'. In its simplest sense that term just means someone from Oklahoma, but for poor people of Guthrie's generation it became pejorative. It was used to belittle and denigrate swathes of worker families who were driven out of the Dust Bowl over to California in search of work. If you've read *The Grapes of Wrath* (and if you haven't, you should), then you'll know all about this.

Woody was born in Okemah, Oklahoma, in 1912. It's fair to say his upbringing didn't exactly go according to plan. By the time he was fourteen, his mother had been admitted to a hospital for the insane and his father, who was also a member of the Ku Klux Klan, was working away in Texas. Woody survived back in Oklahoma by doing odd jobs and sleeping on friends' floors, and knew plenty of hardship. He married young but left his wife and three children to join the great migration west in search of work. Eventually he not only made enough money to send for his family but also got a job playing hillbilly music on LA station KFVD, and wrote a regular column for the Communist newspaper *People's World* between 1939 and 1940.

Clearly Woody Guthrie was a charismatic and persuasive character to have made a life for himself from such difficult beginnings. Those formative experiences and those of the disenfranchised Okies he met, lived and struggled alongside, furnished him with a fervent belief in the need for changes to tackle inequality. Winding up in New York, where alongside his friend Pete Seeger he often organised hootenanny loft parties, he would immortalise many of those thoughts and feelings on the classic *Dust Bowl Ballads* album of 1940.

Slave music of the Deep South had obviously given voice to the struggle of the working man and woman, but Woody may well have been the first to write songs calling for social change and greater equality.

But does a protest song have to be a raucous stripped-down affair performed by a bloke like Guthrie, in a plaid shirt with a battered guitar? Or is there another way to really get your message across – to make protest songs into glossy pop records that will get in the charts and take your message, subliminally perhaps, to millions?

When Frankie Goes To Hollywood released 'Two Tribes' in 1984 its thunderous bass-heavy electronic attack sent it straight to number one. In fact, Frankie would be the first band to have their first three singles hit the top spot since Gerry and the Pacemakers twenty years earlier. To many, it just sounded like a great pop song and club anthem, which it was, and certainly felt a long way from Woody Guthrie, the Dust Bowl Balladeer himself. But it was still expressing the tensions the band observed in the world around them just as Woody had done. At that moment in history, we were at the height of the Cold War with the ever-present nuclear threat hanging over us. 'Two Tribes' brilliantly captured that level of paranoia, with the masterstroke of having narrated segments by the actor Patrick Allen whose apocalyptic gravelly tones had supplied the voice track for the 'Protect and Survive' public information films about how to behave in the event of a nuclear holocaust. 'Hiding under the table' was one of the suggestions. The voice of Ronald Reagan, then American president, was provided by impressionist Chris Barrie (as he did on television in *Spitting Image*) and the video showed a wrestling bout between Reagan and the Russian premier of the time, Konstantin Chernenko. The sleeve portrayed not only images of Reagan, Lenin and Margaret Thatcher but sleeve notes detailing the nuclear capabilities of the relevant powers.

The message could not have been more overt. To some extent this was due to the record company ZTT combining a core team of crack producers and engineers led by Trevor Horn with noted former *New Musical Express* journalist, wordsmith and agent provocateur of the press, Paul Morley. This ensured that the shimmering brilliance of the records they were making – and arguably there were no better produced sounds being made anywhere in the world at that point – would be accompanied by Morley's equally inventive statements. It was the whole package. 'Two Tribes' was just as much a protest song as anything Woody Guthrie had written, but it employed some of the finest minds and latest technologies to create a glittering chart-topper.

A very different example of the protest song wrapped in the shiny packaging of chart success was Bruce Hornsby and the Range's 1986 global hit, 'The Way It Is'. Propelled by a mellifluous piano figure, it became a staple of FM radio and drifted by with a soft rock effortlessness. Yet those paying closer attention to the lyrics would have noticed that some big topics were being confronted. The three verses deal with the inequality between rich and poor, with racial segregation and the Civil Rights Act of 1964. The choruses use the title to imply that some injustices are just the way life is, with an apparent shrug of the shoulders. However, we are urged not to accept this and to see that without struggle and protest, change will never come about. For a catchy, smooth, mid-tempo record that appears to be about just rolling along with life as it is, a far more radical message emerges and therefore it's perhaps no surprise that Tupac Shakur would later sample it for his track 'Changes'. Again, stylistically and production-wise it is a long way from Woody Guthrie but he would surely have been thrilled that part of his legacy had taken such a strong message to so many people across the world. Whether they realised it or not.

Someone who has often paid homage to Woody Guthrie, and has performed acoustically in a similarly stripped-back way, is Bruce Springsteen. Or 'The Boss' as he is unfortunately nicknamed, implying that he has his own reserved parking space and is often away at a conference while his lackeys do all the work. And yet his biggest protest song is one of the most misunderstood in the history of popular music. 'Born in the USA' was the title track of Springsteen's seventh album which would go on to sell over thirty million copies. The cover shows what appears to be a classic Yankee image of a man, Bruce himself photographed from the rear, in Levi's and a white T-shirt, posing in front of the stripes of the

American flag. Some suggested that the figure was urinating on the Stars and Stripes though this has always been denied. Out of one of the rear pockets of the jeans hangs a red baseball cap which would of course later become the headgear of choice for one Donald Trump. Whether this was an intentional reference to Bruce's big patriotic anthem by Trump is unknown, though it seems a little subtle given the latter's usual modus operandi. And if it was intentional then it was a spectacular own goal as this stadium-rocking, air-punching behemoth of a song, which sounds for all the world like an expression of nationalistic pride, is in fact a eulogy for the plight suffered by many Vietnam veterans sent to fight by their country and then left high and dry in the economic recession of the Eighties.

It could not have been less celebratory, if you took a couple of minutes to read the words, despite its sounding for all the world like a soundtrack to a victory march. Which nevertheless it was: it was dragged into service on the campaign trail for the 1984 US election as Ronald Reagan swept to the White House by beating Walter Mondale, taking a record-breaking five hundred and twenty-five electoral college votes out of a possible five hundred and thirty-eight. So for all Bruce's intentions, the misinterpretation of his song was played out for all to see and hear. What would Woody have made of that?

Protest songs may be forged from the hardships of the beatnik outsider, but perhaps they are at their most potent when performed by the biggest and most successful acts there are. Pioneering women artists like Odetta and

Nina Simone had never been shy of confronting burning issues in their music. In 2003 the Dixie Chicks attracted widespread opprobrium, and indeed death threats, for publicly criticising the Iraq War and expressing their disdain for sitting president George W. Bush. These themes, and their reactions to how they were treated, were dealt with on the 2006 album *Taking the Long Way*, and most explicitly on the single 'Not Ready to Make Nice'. Despite the controversy, the track went on to go platinum and win Grammy Awards the following year, among them for Song of the Year, proving that they had many supporters as well as detractors. Once more the message had emphatically hit home.

In 2004 one of America's biggest stadium-filling bands released a concept album that they genuinely hoped would influence the thinking of a generation. A lofty ideal perhaps but Green Day were huge, with millions of kids hanging on their every word. *American Idiot* was a concept record but rather like a previous era when Vietnam dominated the public consciousness, this was released when George W. Bush and the Iraq War were, as the Dixie Chicks knew all too well, paramount in people's minds. For a punk-pop group to take on the biggest subjects is praiseworthy if perhaps foolhardy, but Green Day did manage to capture the fears and neuroses of those times. In fact you could make a strong case for saying that if protest music should have a timeless universality and deal with topics that seem perennial, this album could just have easily been made after the election of Donald Trump in 2016, and in a way it's a pity that

Woody Guthrie isn't still around to witness Trump's America as one imagines he would have found plenty to write about.

Of course the biggest group the world has ever seen were The Beatles, and with the confidence and freedom that brought them to stardom, it's instructive to know that gazing down on the world from their lofty pedestal, the first song they recorded for 'The White Album' was 'Revolution'. Early 1968 was a tempestuous time and John Lennon was well-aware of it. On 17 March a huge anti-Vietnam march advanced on the American Embassy on Grosvenor Square in London. There were uprisings in Poland the same month, followed by the well-documented riots in Paris in May. Lennon was clearly identifying with the struggles and yet seems, perhaps having experimented with transcendental meditation, to be unconvinced of the need for violent protest. He was a dyed-in-the-wool 'make love not war' man whose idea of radical direct action was to take to his bed but no one could say he wasn't genuine in looking to a higher power to bring world peace. It was worth a shot, but what would Woody have thought of eschewing the Molotov cocktails in favour of cocktails on room service at the Amsterdam Hilton? But John was one of the four biggest pop stars in the world and, without needing to, used his position to try to preach understanding and comradeship – and what's wrong with that? He had no need to do it. The history of The Beatles to that point hadn't led people to expect guidance on the burning issues of the day, but an increasingly politicised Lennon believed it was something he had to do.

Others had a more radical view of how change was going to come about. Writer, musician and activist Chicagoan Gil Scott-Heron, whose father was the first black player for Glasgow Celtic FC, may well have taken note of Lennon's utterings about revolution from his privileged position and the associating press scrum that came with it, but he was equally sure that when it came, 'The Revolution Will Not Be Televised', the title of his classic track from 1971. Scott-Heron was a visionary and an influential thinker. Chuck D of Public Enemy, who released their own call to arms 'Fight The Power' in 1989, said on hearing of his death: 'We do what we do and how we do because of you.' Like Guthrie, Gil Scott-Heron's sincerity and principles are not to be questioned but he was sadly wrong in a key area. The right-wing establishment may well have controlled all media outlets including television during the civil rights movement of the late Sixties and for many decades afterwards, so Gil was right for a long time. And like the rest of us, he can have had no inkling of how social media would change the world. Nowadays anyone can upload content to a global audience whenever they like and so we may not know if there's going to be a revolution – or if there is, when it will be – but what we do know for sure is that when it happens it will definitely be televised. Or livestreamed if you prefer.

Woody Guthrie's *Dust Bowl Ballads* dealt with universal themes but were inspired by the experiences

and injustices meted out to a specific group of unfortu-
nates at a particular point in time and many protest
songs follow this blueprint. Rather like John Lennon,
Bono's statements and actions can sometimes leave him
open to cries of derision but again, no one can knock
his determination to use his platform as one of the
world's biggest rock stars to highlight social issues. U2's
first albums, 1980's *Boy* and its follow-up *October*,
showed no overt sign that a political agenda was perco-
lating in their work and so when 1983's *War* opened
with 'Sunday Bloody Sunday' it came as something of a
surprise. A desperate plea for pacifism in the wake of
the unspeakable violence that occurred in Derry on
30 January 1972, it has something Lennonesque about
it, and one suspects that many fans of Bono's band, as
quite possibly disciples of The Beatles had, would rather
Bono had left the politics behind. But here is one of the
central points of the pop star protest singer: by expressing
your view, which some might say is overly simplistic,
you are giving your huge audience the chance to disagree
with you and in theory walk away. That's a bravery of
sorts which Woody Guthrie could have admired, though
I don't have him down as a quintessential U2 fan. I
could be wrong of course.

I think he'd have liked the Manic Street Preachers,
though. Since their very earliest days they wrapped themselves in revolutionary imagery and had a passion,
fervour and anger, even if it wasn't always clear what
they were angry about. However, as their focus became
ever sharper, so many of their songs took specific

moments from history and gave them wider resonance through the steely lyrical gaze of Nicky Wire. A case in point would be a track from their 1998 album *This Is My Truth, Tell Me Yours*, a title which is in itself a quote from Aneurin 'Nye' Bevan, the lifelong democratic socialist son of a miner who was the founding father of the National Health Service. 'If You Tolerate This Your Children Will Be Next' was inspired by Welsh volunteers and miners who joined the International Brigades to fight against General Franco in the Spanish Civil War of 1936–39, but there is a universality to the message. It's a classic thin-end-of-the-wedge sentiment. Sometimes you have to fight for something because if you don't things will be even worse for the children you leave behind. Sometimes there are lines drawn in the sand that cannot be crossed without one hell of a fight. And the other marvellous thing to note is that this was a UK number one single. Talk about getting your message out there. It is also, and this is entirely irrelevant to what we're talking about but pleasing nonetheless, the longest title (without brackets) of any British chart topper so well done, lads.

Whether Woody Guthrie wanted to be number one in the charts we will never know. It's pretty certain he wouldn't have worn a feather boa and leopardskin-print frock on stage like Nicky Wire, but it's fair to say that all protest singers are to some extent look-at-me egomaniacs. You have to believe you've got something that's worth people hearing or you wouldn't stand up and do it. If Woody Guthrie didn't want to be idolised and get off with girls, he could have stayed writing his column and preaching to the converted in *People's World*.

But a response to events going on around you is the bedrock of the protest song. A track like the Sex Pistols' 'God Save The Queen' might seem like a simple republican battle cry but John Lydon has repeatedly pointed out that it is a view of the disenfranchised and dispossessed of our nation who nevertheless broke out the bunting for the Silver Jubilee of 1977. The Specials' synchronicitous 'Ghost Town' hit number one in 1981, the same weekend that the police used CS gas on rioters in Toxteth. Their subsequent outfit The Special AKA, meanwhile, scored a huge hit in 1984 calling for the release of Nelson Mandela, while four years earlier Peter Gabriel's 'Biko' (featured on his third album) had turned the spotlight on the plight of Steve Biko who had died in police custody in South Africa in 1977.

There have been many protest songs that have been concerned with specific sets of events with messages that have been pumped out across the wirelesses of the world, and yet some of the most enduring examples do seem to have a less specific, dreamier simplicity to them. It's become quite fashionable to sneer at John Lennon for 'Imagine', where he sings about relinquishing all wealth from the confines of his imposing pure white mansion, and yet I think this is unfair. He's not, I believe, trying to say that he himself hasn't been somehow ensnared by rampant materialism, but simply encouraging us to think about the abstract possibility of a new world. It is an exercise in the power, or indeed futility, of positive thinking.

When I was undergoing my treatment for cancer I was constantly told to keep a positive frame of mind as the alternative is to sink into depression and despair. You have to keep believing that you will get through this and that a better life is possible. There were times when I could hardly get out of bed, barely ate anything and was certainly in no position to work or do anything useful for my family. Thankfully, I did get through it and life feels like a blessing every day now, and I think that Lennon was simply articulating this on a grand scale. We have to believe in our capacity to change and reach for something higher.

Similarly, Patti Smith sings on 'People Have the Power', from her 1988 *Dream of Life* album, that we can collectively 'wrestle the world from fools'. Well, I guess sometimes we can and sometimes we can't but what a precious concept to remember that is. The great Sam Cooke was sure that 'A Change is Going to Come'. Universal truths endure. Even Woody Guthrie's most obvious torchbearer Bob Dylan was moved by the Cuban Missile Crisis to sing 'A Hard Rain's Gonna Fall' in 1963 and yet the meaning of the song utterly transcends that moment in history. He may be talking about acid rain, he may not be, but the song is full of imagery that can be applied to all kinds of situations. It is apocalyptic and as relevant today whether used in reference to seismic financial, political, human or climactic change. There is in a sense always going to be the next 'hard rain' and it will certainly fall on some of us.

Dylan is one of many people who has covered Guthrie's

'This Land is Your Land', as have Bruce Springsteen, Peter, Paul and Mary, The Kingston Trio, The New Christy Minstrels, The Seekers, Connie Francis, Johnny Logan and that stalwart of the leftist struggle Bing Crosby. Woody wrote the lyrics in 1940 to a tune called 'When the World's on Fire' that he'd heard performed by the Carter Family, and the song was added to the National Recording Registry by the Library of Congress in 2002. The words refer to specific places, and yet its message, like all the songs listed above, has remained universal – not least in its dealings with trespass and a 'big high wall'. Now where have we heard about that recently?

18

It's Got to Be Perfect

This book has been devoted to exploring and recog-
nising significant moments when something changed
on the rock and roll superhighway. We've stopped off
at intersections where new directions were taken by
innovators, risk-takers and chancers, creating bands
whose influence would be felt for ever. So it stands to
reason that if someone managed to create the perfect
template for the all-important pop group, both musically
and visually, they would be standing at a junction all of
their own. So what makes the perfect pop group? And
has anyone done it?

Well, for a start there can only be four members: vocals,
guitar, bass, drums. That's it. It's to do with the symmetry
of the thing. The drums go in the middle at the back,
the singer stands at front centre, and the guitarist and
bass player take a side each. It's just the way it is, so
apologies to the Rolling Stones who've got one member
too many. With all due respect to Brian Jones, whose

band it was initially, with Mick and Keith just backed by the inscrutable and insouciant Bill Wyman and Charlie Watts, they would have been a shoe-in.

The relatively low-profile rhythm section is also an essential part of the structure and so The Smiths, U2 and Kasabian may be approaching the perfect template – though there were four other chaps who got it even more right than they did. Although the drummer is allowed to be a nutcase as long as the bassist is quiet enough for both of them, which brings The Who into the picture. The Beatles fall down here because if they were going to be the fabbest four then George, the quiet one, would have had to be on bass to stand at the back next to the goofy tub-thumper.

A narcissistic preening frontman is also a requirement and so all the bands mentioned so far qualify on that score, as do Led Zeppelin. In Jimmy Page, Zeppelin also have the guitarist mastermind who ever so slightly resents the attention the lead singer gets even if he doesn't admit it. He, or she of course, thinks they've put in all the hours of writing and production only for someone with better hair to steal the limelight come showtime. So Led Zep score very highly here, because they have the rumbustious drummer, the reticent bassist, the Machiavellian guitarist and the caterwauling rock god. They win. Except they're not a pop group. They're a rock band, so the search goes on. Same for The Who. And Black Sabbath.

The Monkees look ideal in pictures and made great records but it all goes wrong when you see them play.

Or at least pretend to play. Micky Dolenz often sings from behind the drums, looking distinctly unconvincing, while Davy Jones – the pretty one – stands at the front with maracas. Half of the band couldn't really play and any classic four-piece has to be able to do that. They also have to have been mates for years, preferably since high school, and the Monkees came together through an audition process. Great pop bands also have to look like they belong together and have, by a process of osmosis, learnt to dress individually but on a common theme or set of rules. Again, the Monkees fall down because they match too painstakingly, having been put into identical shirts by the wardrobe department. The Red Hot Chili Peppers come unstuck here too, because their extrovert multicoloured playsuited and occasionally naked bass player Flea contrasts too starkly with whichever guitarist they've got at the time, who always looks like a particularly grungy tree surgeon.

The Stone Roses have it about right, though bass player Mani is more animated than non-macho guitar hero John Squire on the other side, which lets them down a bit. You could say the same thing about Bernard Sumner and Peter Hook in Joy Division. Blur also come pretty close, though lead singer Damon Albarn sometimes played keyboards which spoils it completely. You can't have organs and synthesizers cluttering up the middle of the stage at the front. It's just wrong. Queen of course tick every box here. They have the preeniest frontman, with his piano safely off towards the wings of the stage, the prettiest drummer, the noodliest guitarist and the quietest bass player. In fact bass player, John Deacon, has become even quieter since the band ended. He's papped occasionally wearing an anorak with a rolled-up newspaper under his arm and says absolutely nothing in public ever – though there are tales that he is still involved in helping them count the money. But then again, all that operatic stuff gives them ideas above their station. A classic four-piece pop group should only play classic three-minute tracks. Leave the intricate stuff to the prog rock guys. This, of course, was one of the main thrusts of punk and that's why all the classic punk bands like the Sex Pistols, The Clash, The Damned, Buzzcocks and the Heartbreakers had four members. It's about giving you the bare bones with no embellishment. Sometimes the bare bones are all you need. Talking of which . . .

We begin with sixteen bars of buzzsaw guitar, bass and drums in straight 4/4 timing. At twenty-two seconds, the bass and guitar drop out and a chant of 'Hey Ho Let's Go' begins. The bass returns on thunderous root notes at twenty-eight seconds in. The guitar comes back at thirty-one. The vocals of the verse kick off at thirty-three seconds, taking us to the chorus at fifty-five. At one minute and six seconds we get the same verse again with another chorus at one minute and twenty-eight seconds. There is no solo or middle eight. The same verse appears a third time at one thirty-nine before the chant, bass and guitar sequence returns to wrap the song up at an exquisite two minutes and eleven seconds. The song is 'Blitzkrieg Bop' by the Ramones and it is perfect in every way.

And I'm glad about that because I'd been fascinated by the Ramones from reading about them in the *New Musical Express* before I had heard them. That was the way it was in those days. We had to read about new bands and then imagine what they might sound like as they certainly weren't going to get played on the radio. Well, not unless John Peel picked it up. We couldn't even listen to their records because they often hadn't been released, and even if they had, the shops in Bolton wouldn't stock them. That meant that even if you'd managed to save up enough pocket money to purchase the disc – and unheard, that was quite an expensive leap of faith – the prized artefact still wouldn't arrive for several weeks. I discussed this with Pet Shop Boy Neil Tennant, who used to work for *Smash Hits*, and he was rather wistfully nostalgic for the almost magical quality that was bestowed on a record, and the sense of anticipation, wonder and gratification that came with finally being able to place it on the turntable.

When I eventually heard the Ramones, inevitably on Peel's show on late night Radio One, it was a crushing disappointment. Lying in bed under my swirly-patterned yellow and lime green single duvet cover, Peel played 'I Wanna Be Your Boyfriend'. I grew to love this song and its pure pop sensibility, but having expected an incendiary barrage of noise, its gentleness came as an unwelcome surprise. It didn't feel like it was breaking any new ground. On 'Blitzkrieg Bop', though, it was clear something important was happening and I adored it instantly.

The Ramones were buddies from the Forest Hills area of the New York borough of Queens and played the last of two thousand two hundred and sixty-three concerts in 1996. *Rolling Stone* magazine put them at number twenty-six in their chart of the one hundred most important artists of all time. In 2002 *Spin* magazine had them as the second greatest band ever after The Beatles. Now, even though I'm making a very strong case for the Ramones here – I bloody love the Ramones – this is patently ridiculous, but it does show that there are plenty of people who think they're as important as I do.

So let's have a look at them and see why they might just be the perfect pop group. First, there are four of them: Johnny, Joey, Tommy and DeeDee. They all had the surname Ramone. Except they didn't. They weren't really brothers at all but adopted the name at the insistence of bassist DeeDee who got it from Paul McCartney's pseudonym in The Silver Beatles, and a name he often checked into hotels under, of Paul Ramon. Their real names don't matter because they will always be immortalised as the Ramones. Google them if it bothers you.

So they had the same name and they looked like a gang. They looked like the same guys they were when they had hung out together before the band was even formed. Their image is a design classic and something of a cliché now, but it wasn't then as they did it first. Well, maybe it was a take on the James Dean blueprint, but they made it their own. They each wore a black leather jacket, T-shirt, drainpipe jeans and scuffed white plimsolls. Not trainers. Pumps. Crucially though, their jackets are not identical like the Monkees' jackets would have been. On the front cover of their debut album of 1976, Johnny is on the left in a biker jacket whereas DeeDee on the far right has gone for a blouson. Joey has a rip in the right knee of his jeans but none of the others do. Tommy's T-shirt doesn't cover his belly button. Everyone else's does. It's not a uniform. It's a dress code you interpret for yourself.

One of their most famous songs is 1977's 'Rockaway Beach'. This is a real beach in Queens which you can reach from downtown New York by taking the 'A' train, as immortalised by Billy Strayhorn in 1939 when he composed 'Take the "A" Train' which became the Duke Ellington Orchestra's signature tune. So take the 'A' and switch to the 'S' at Broad Channel and you'll find your way easily enough to Rockaway Beach, which has in its time been home to a lot of the Big Apple's well-to-do. The Ramones apparently often used to stroll along the shoreline here and I've always wondered whether in hot weather their garb restrictions were relaxed so you might come across them strolling four abreast in leather jackets, T-shirts, plimsolls and Speedos. The Ramones in budgie smugglers. It's quite an image.

In a way, visually at least, the band breaks down into two pairs. Joey and Tommy in the middle are wearing sunglasses and have shoulder length 'grebo' hair whereas the wing men DeeDee and Johnny are shades-less and have Byrds/Brian Jones-style bowl cuts. Once more, the symmetry. A pudding basin on each side of the stage. In another cliché, but again only because they kind of invented it, they're standing in front of a brick wall with graffitied concrete below. And above them on the cover is the title of the album: *Ramones*. That's it. One word. Sometimes it's all you need.

And what an album it is. There are fourteen tracks, all originals except a cover of Chris Montez's 'Let's Dance', with the longest being two minutes and thirty-five seconds and the shortest one minute thirty. The whole thing clocks in at a whisker over twenty-nine minutes. The opening assault of 'Blitzkrieg Bop' sets the tone and DeeDee has said that they wanted a chant because they were very much taken with the shouted spelling out of 'S-A-T-U-R-D-A-Y' on the hit single 'Saturday Night' by the Bay City Rollers. (The Rollers, despite having a good tartan dress gimmick and interchangeable haircuts, can't be the perfect group because there were five of them.) But the Ramones just wanted to create a song that captured the excitement of seeing your favourite band live. And seeing the Ramones live was exhilarating. The pummelling beat was relentless, the root bass notes stomach-churning, the vocals staccato and the barre chords propelled with such force by Johnny that he often bled over the scratch plate of his fifty dollar single pick-up Mosrite guitar which he carried to gigs on the subway in a shopping bag in the early days. DeeDee would count each song in over the decaying last chord of the previous number. It was an all-out assault.

The Ramones looked great and sounded great and managed to distil rock and roll down to its base elements. Adornment was unnecessary if you had great songs bashed out with enough attitude and belief, and that's why they're just about the most perfect pop group there has ever been. They created a blueprint for stripped-down rock and roll that has never been bettered.

You'll have noticed that this chapter isn't very long, but sometimes the bare bones are all you need.

19

The Concept

The world of popular music can be divided into the BD and AD periods. That is to say before and after, or anno if you prefer, *The Dark Side of the Moon*. For the first time the esoteric world of the noodling prog-rockers, if that's what Pink Floyd are, became just as huge a deal as any of the glam and glittery pop stars of the day. Perhaps more than any record in history, it stands at a crossroads where it becomes clear that with the right record at the right time, anyone can become massively successful. You don't even have to be pretty or smile. Even those who were previously considered as being consigned to the underground for eternity. It is, put succinctly, a game-changer.

There's probably not much I can tell you about this classic album that you don't already know. It was released in March 1973, and though it only reached number two here, it is the seventh best-selling album in the UK after Queen's *Greatest Hits*, *ABBA Gold*, *Sgt. Pepper's Lonely*

Hearts Club Band, Adele's *21*, *Cider-Drinking Favourites* by Adge Cutler and the Wurzels and Michael Jackson's *Thriller*. To be honest I've regurgitated that top six from memory, so it's possible I've got something wrong but no matter. You get the idea. *The Dark Side of the Moon* has sold shedloads of copies. Over forty-five million. It went to number one in the States for a solitary week but then stayed on the charts for seven hundred and forty-one weeks between 1973 and 1988. How gutted must they have been to finally crash out of the hit parade. One can imagine the conversation:

'Hello, Nick Mason speaking.'
'Nick, it's Dave.'
'Dave who?'
'Gilmour, you idiot.'
'Oh, alright, Dave? How's your houseboat?'
'Never mind that. I've got some bad news.'
'Oh, cripes. Roger's not coming back, is he?'
'No, but we're not in the charts any more.'
'Bugger. And I just bought another Ferrari.'
'Right. Will you let Rick know?'
'Rick who?'
'Oh, never mind. I'll do it.'

When *Dark Side* was released I was fourteen, and as a white, middle-class grammar-school boy it was practically illegal not to own it. It might as well have been on the National Curriculum. Everybody I was mates with knew every note and word of that album, from

218

the opening heartbeats to the same sound fading away at the other end. We knew that it was a concept album concerning the things that sent people mad: passing of time, money, greed, conflict and mental illness itself. We knew it was in some way inspired by the psychological struggles of their previous leader, Syd Barrett, and his well-documented descent into some private mental hell. Actually, I probably didn't really know all that at the time, now I think about it. These days every fourteen-year-old is coached in mindfulness but back then I was more likely to be thinking about whether it would be a good soundtrack to some canoodling with Hilary Wardle if my mum would let her come up to my room to sample the sonic delights of my prized Boots Audio Hi-Fi.

A day at school didn't go by without seeing someone with that album sleeve under their arm, with its beautifully bold and simple image of the refracting prism. And it came with some associated paraphernalia. There were postcards of pyramids and some pyramid stickers and, best of all, some pyramid posters. These went straight up on my wall alongside posters of Peter Fonda and Dennis Hopper riding their choppers in *Easy Rider*, Rupert the Bear, of whom I remain a committed fan, and Olivia Newton-John, who had a nice face. I did eventually meet Olivia Newton-John in January of 2017 at the Celtic Connections festival in Glasgow. She still had a nice face and even when I told her that I'd had to replace her picture in my bedroom with Pink Floyd before Hilary got there she didn't seem to take offence, though her PR person did step in to say she had to be going to a live radio interview at exactly that point. Funny that.

Hilary and I did eventually see the Floyd perform their masterpiece at Manchester's Palace Theatre on 10 December 1974. We sat in the upper circle while they played early versions of 'Sheep' and 'Dogs', which would later appear on the *Animals* album, before unveiling the then unreleased majesty of 'Shine on You Crazy Diamond'. Then there was an interval where we couldn't get served at the bar and so had to make do with a bag of Uncle Joe's Mint Balls I'd brought with me, because I always did know how to spoil a girl. We then took our seats for the second half and they did the whole of *The Dark Side of the Moon* as a continuous piece, which of course it was always intended to be. The only gap on the album version was when you had to take the vinyl off to turn it over. Each side was a continuous soundscape. And up there in 'the gods' we were afforded the perfect view of Floyd's famed visuals. Their lights and projections onto a large circular screen were way beyond anything we'd seen when we went to gigs by bands at Bolton Institute of Technology and the whole tableau was so impressive that it didn't seem to matter that you couldn't make out the musicians clearly. This to me has always been one of the Floyd masterstrokes. That the whole show was the thing and not just the players as personalities. They didn't look especially pretty and certainly didn't smile.

To top things off they did the epic 'Echoes' as the encore.

Amazing then that a concept album about mental illness made by four blokes seemingly devoid of charisma could become one the biggest-selling and most enduring albums in recording history. At one time, a German pressing plant was turning out nothing but *Dark Side* twenty-four hours a day, such was the demand. Pink Floyd, and it's hard not to think that bands like Radiohead would become cognisant of this, proved that you didn't have to try to be commercial to be commercial.

The concept album is often something to be approached with caution, though many progressive rock bands considered it something that they had to do to prove they were 'serious'. The Moody Blues mixed songs and orchestral passages on the 1967 album *Days of Future Passed*, generally accepted to be the first British concept album. It was basically a song suite, including 'Nights In White Satin', which dealt with the everyday life of man. Wow. Of all the subjects to pick, that sounds pretty dull. Perhaps mindful of that, the Small Faces released their concept piece the following year. *Ogdens' Nut Gone Flake* was named after the tobacco that came in distinctive round tins, and original copies of the vinyl, and subsequently CD, were issued in similar metal packaging, ensuring that they often rolled off the shelves of the record shop and clattered to the floor. The hero of *Ogdens' Nut Gone Flake* is one Happiness Stan who is on a quest to find the missing half of the moon. Not the dark side but the missing side. The spoken sections are undertaken by a chap called Stanley Unwin who was a bit of a national treasure at the time. He had his own brand of nonsensical bastardised English which led him to numerous television and radio appearances and helped propel *Ogden's* to number one in the charts. Again, it seems amazing in retrospect, but I guess the Small Faces were just so big at that time people would buy anything they chose to put out and the album does contain some classic tracks like 'Lazy Sunday' and 'Song of a Baker'.

Also in 1968 The Kinks quite brilliantly focused on what it meant to be quintessentially English on *The Kinks Are the Village Green Preservation Society*, and then to round things off that December The Pretty Things' lead singer Phil May got all progtastic when he utilised his own short story about the life of a geezer called Sebastian F. Sorrow to form the basis of the LP *S.F. Sorrow*, during which we go from birth to death via the subconscious and the underworld. Well, why not, eh?

Sometimes the conceptual nature of the beast seemed to overwhelm the musical side, often leading to double albums to try and tell the whole story. A classic case in point would be *The Lamb Lies Down on Broadway* by Genesis. Released in November 1974, it tells the story of . . . well, I'm reluctant to even go here as, again, based on a short story by their lead singer, Peter Gabriel, the narrative is abstract to say the least. It concerns Rael, a Puerto Rican youth living in New York who, rather like Sebastian Sorrow, seems to take an allegorical journey through the sewers ostensibly to find his brother John but along the way journeys to the centre of the subconscious. Or something. It may be Jungian, it may have something to do with *West Side Story* or

Pilgrim's Progress, but it is a sprawling melange of wordage and musical meanderings. Along the way Rael meets enough odd characters to provide Doctor Who with adversaries for many years, most notably the Slippermen who were about ten feet tall and resembled frogmen who'd risen too quickly and got the bends, resulting in huge pustulous warts breaking out all over their skin. Never a good look. Peter Gabriel of course had a full outfit made, though it led to consternation within the ranks when the other band members realised the wearing of it left him more or less unable to sing properly.

The tensions of recording and performing *The Lamb* led to Gabriel leaving the band. These hugely ambitious projects can take their toll. It's probably not one of their works you're familiar with, but in 1969 the Bee Gees of all people recorded a double concept album called *Odessa.* It concerned the loss of a fictional ship in 1899 and caused so much internal strife that Robin Gibb left his brothers for a time after completing it.

In the Genesis camp the rest of the band seemed to resent the attention heaped upon Gabriel and reportedly grew frustrated at his struggle to come up with the torrent of lyrics as required. At one point Phil Collins is said to have suggested they should release an instrumental album though that idea was rapidly quashed. Bassist Mike Rutherford had apparently suggested an alternative concept based on Antoine de Saint-Exupéry's *The Little Prince,* but Gabriel was quickly dismissive of that.

I saw Genesis perform the whole shebang for two nights running in April 1975 – again at Manchester's Palace Theatre. Being a massive fan of the band and young and impressionable, I thought it was incredible. Apparently it baffled American audiences, not least because the band – or Peter at least – insisted on performing it in full before the album had even been released over there. You'd have to say that that was asking quite a lot of the audience, on reflection.

I suppose how much of the concept you need to understand depends on how much you enjoy the music. We loved the idea that Peter Gabriel was all arty-farty and lost in his own world, as long as Collins drove them with his particular percussive fire and Steve Hackett unfurled his labyrinthine guitar lines. With Yes's *Tales of Topographic Oceans* we didn't need to have a working knowledge of the Hindu texts known as the shastras that had evidently formed the basic inspiration for the four side-long compositions. We just luxuriated in the scale and ambition and indeed pretentiousness of the thing. We were serious-minded adolescents and pop music was for little kids. Well, and girls, so when we went out we still danced to Van McCoy like everyone else.

But this willingness on behalf of artists and record companies to experiment on a grand scale seems to me something that is sadly lacking these days. It is extraordinary when you look at an album like Jethro Tull's *Aqualung* from 1971. The character on the cover is actually called Aqualung as his voice resembles someone croaking through that apparatus. He is homeless and certainly looks like a Fagin who has let himself go a bit, a look often adopted by the band themselves. Dapper they most certainly weren't. The concept seems to involve the life of this character but has also been said to concern the distinction between religion and God. It's always hard to tell with these things though, and leader Ian Anderson has subsequently denied that it's a concept album at all. Nevertheless it is incredible that a band who looked like they had come to empty a cesspit, and who were named after the inventor of the seed drill, could release an album about a tramp and sell seven million copies. Sadly I just can't see any way that could happen now. The world seems a bit less fun when you think of it like that, doesn't it?

But if you think the concept album is pretty much exclusively the domain of the prog-rocker you'd be wrong. People who you wouldn't expect to approach something like this in a million years turn up and surprise you. Consider the fact that as early as 1960, at the start of the sexual revolution, a long-player called *Wild Is Love* was released, documenting a narrator's attempts to pick up women. Spoiler alert – he gets lucky in the end. Sounds faintly ghastly but you'll be astounded to know that it was by Nat King Cole.

In 1979 Barbra Streisand released a concept album on the subject of water. It was called *Wet*, which was also the first and last word sung on the album. It included a version of the deeply conceptual Bobby Darin classic 'Splish Splash I Was Having A Bath'. Well, that would certainly involve water so the concept seems altogether more focused than *The Lamb Lies Down On Broadway*. And, bizarrely, Sarah Brightman also made a water-themed album in 1993 with *Dive*.

One can only imagine the looks on the faces of the record company executives in the boardroom when Janet Jackson told them that the follow-up to her 1986 *Control* album, which broke her around the world and sold over ten million copies, was going to be called *Janet Jackson's Rhythm Nation 1814* and would concern racism, poverty and substance abuse. She went ahead and made it anyway, and in Tull-stylee was massively successful, going to number one in the *Billboard* charts.

Even Mariah Carey had a crack at one in 2014. It was a journey through soul in all its many forms and was called, in a title that beautifully brought together all the elements of that rich cultural heritage and certainly didn't accentuate the artist herself, *Me. I am Mariah . . . The Elusive Chanteuse*. Elusive indeed.

It's also worth noting that in 2005 a concept album about what it was like to be a twenty-something girl living in London came out. It was called *Chemistry* and was by Girls Aloud. That certainly seems more surprising than when Saruman himself, Christopher Lee, released a symphonic metal concept album in 2010 about the first Holy Roman emperor called *Charlemagne: By the Sword and the Cross*. I mean, who wouldn't want to go and see that rather than Ed Sheeran again, right?

Some concept albums do seem doomed from the start, and a classic example of this was inadvisably allowed out in 1975. Serge Gainsbourg does of course have form where scandal is concerned and was what used to be called, with a Gallic shrug, a bit of a ladies' man. I suppose these days we'd be more likely to say something like lecherous old pervert. #MeToo. In 1966 he wrote a song for the popular yé-yé chanteuse France Gall. A proven hit artist, she scored again with his song 'Les Sucettes' which translates as 'Lollipops'. It turned out to be about licking and sucking something else entirely. In 1969 he had a worldwide success with his explicit duet with Jane Birkin 'Je t'aime . . . moi non plus', despite its being banned in several countries. Two years later, he unveiled a concept album titled *Histoire de Melody Nelson* in which he threw himself wholeheartedly into a Lolita-style scenario. In the mid-Eighties he again caused a scandal when he put out a record with his daughter Charlotte called 'Lemon Incest'.

Despite, or perhaps because of, this track record he was still revered as a great writer and artist in his native France and often appeared on chat shows. One notable appearance came on the Michel Drucker show, which went out live and nationwide on a Saturday night. Visibly drunk, Gainsbourg is seated next to Whitney Houston, with whom he is much taken. When he makes a comment to her *en Français*, Whitney looks to the host for a translation. Michel gives what might be called a sanitised version of what was actually expressed. Serge takes exception to this and, to leave la Houston in no doubt of his feelings, translates himself verbatim and says: 'I said, "I want to fuck her".' Quite the charmer.

But even knowing all this about him, and the leeway he was evidently given by a largely adoring French media and public, surely someone could have suggested that a Nazi-themed concept album was a bad idea. He released it, though, in 1975. It is called *Rock Around the Bunker* and the opening track is 'Nazi Rock'. Who could possibly object?

Someone else who likes a concept project is prog-rock anecdotalist and maestro of the mellotron and mini-moog Lord Rick of Wakeman. He played on the aforementioned *Tales of Topographic Oceans* of course, but opened his solo account in 1973 with *The Six Wives of Henry VIII* where each wife was given her own dedicated piece. He followed this up the next year with *Journey to the Centre of the Earth* and, nothing if not prolific, took only another twelve months to unveil *The Myths and Legends of King Arthur and the Knights of the Round Table*, which he staged as part gig, part medieval pageant. On ice. Sadly he seemed to tire of the big concept piece after that, though I did once offer him a way back. When he appeared on a radio show I was co-hosting with Marc Riley, we suggested a prog trio with me on drums, Marc on bass and the Wakemeister tinkling the old ivories. To avoid any arguments, we said we would name the band strictly alphabetically and so in an Emerson, Lake & Palmer manner we would be immortalised as Radcliffe, Riley & Wakeman. The concept we took to him was called 'Journey Back from the Centre of the Earth to Merseyway Bus Station in Stockport'. He said he didn't rulc it out, but he's been not ruling it out for a very long time now.

For the most part concept albums have remained an engaging sideshow in the history of rock and pop, though occasional masterpieces do break through. My favourite album of all is a concept album: *The Rise and Fall of Ziggy Stardust and the Spiders from Mars* by David Bowie. But the towering achievement of this peculiar sub-genre will forever be *The Dark Side of the Moon*. Well, that's what I told my mum I was explaining to Hilary Wardle in my bedroom anyway.

20

Lady of the Canyon

S pending several hours of the limited time I had available in Los Angeles in a private clinic in Beverly Hills when one of my daughters developed an eye infection wasn't exactly ideal, schedule- or budget-wise, so the time I got to spend up at Laurel Canyon was limited. It didn't really matter though as the place has an atmosphere that hits you instantly. And for me, not necessarily in an entirely positive way.

The canyon runs between West Hollywood and the East San Fernando Valley, snaking around the celebrated thoroughfares of Sunset Boulevard and Mulholland Drive. The roads are narrow and steep and are scarred from the waters rushing down from the mountains when the rainstorms break. The buildings range from eccentric kooky mansions to little more than rustic shacks, and it wouldn't be a surprise if you suddenly passed the houses lived in by the Munsters or the Addams Family. Perhaps I had in my mind Charles Manson and his 'family' cruising those steep sleepy slopes and creepy-crawling some of the hipster hangouts, but the place has a blissed-out feel with just a tiny undercurrent of something more sinister. It's kind of witchy, somehow. There have been plenty of murders and mysterious fires there, but I guess that where lots of drug deals are done, and whacked-out space cadets smoke copious amounts of dope in wooden buildings, that's more or less inevitable. Fire hazard awareness tends not to be high on the agenda.

But it has always been a hangout for the cooler end of the celebrity community ever since Harry Houdini had a big gaff there in the Twenties. It is close to Hollywood and everything that's going on, but it is also a world apart. A hippie enclave, if you like. Some of the people who have lived there include Marlon Brando, James Dean, Frank Zappa, Dennis Hopper, The Mamas and the Papas, Dusty Springfield, Linda Ronstadt, Brian Wilson, Joni Mitchell – and Graham Nash, for whom the terraced streets of Salford must have seemed a very long way away. Nash was in fact an easy convert to the Californian dream, having looked down from a plane while travelling with The Hollies and seen all the swimming pools laid out behind the homes and thinking that it looked better than rainy Manchester in the Sixties. You can see his point, and even though it was a snap judgement it turned out to be right for him because he never did come 'home'. Mind you, he did manage to get shacked up with Joni so that must have helped.

You can imagine the kinds of parties you might have

been invited to, if you were one of the in-crowd. It was an age of drugs and permissiveness, which tend to mix particularly well with swimming pools and sunshine, and such was the all-pervading vibe emanating from that idiosyncratic little haven, there came to be music which was described as having a Laurel Canyon feel or sound. Everybody knew what that meant. It was unhurried, had glistening harmonies, it connected with personal feelings, and it didn't try too hard to be a hit. If the living was easy then so were the tunes.

Into this scene stepped someone about to make one of the greatest albums of all time, but who had lived a very different life up to that point. Carole King was born in Manhattan in 1942 where her mother worked as a teacher and her father for the New York City Fire Department. They could have perhaps used his expertise down in Laurel Canyon, where the next conflagration was never far away. From her earliest years, Carole had been fascinated by her mum's piano and it was discovered from the age of four that she had perfect, or absolute, pitch, which means the ability to recognise notes without any tonal references; an amazing natural ability, especially to those of us who find it difficult to sing in tune, even when all the instruments are audible.

There was clearly a pretty formidable musical mind taking shape in the young Carole and so piano lessons duly ensued, for which she'd have to sit on the phone book to reach the keyboard. An early developer, by the age of fourteen she was regularly taking the subway to Brooklyn touting her music to publishers, although she

233

struggled to write completed songs as she didn't really do lyrics. This all changed when she met another New York Jewish kid at college. Gerry Goffin was three years older than Carole and together they would become one of the most successful songwriting partnerships in history. In fact, John Lennon once said that he wanted him and Paul to be the Goffin and King of England.

Life seemed to have moved pretty fast for the co-writing prodigies: they became romantically as well as musically and lyrically intertwined and Carole was pregnant with their first daughter by the time she was seventeen and Gerry just twenty. Notwithstanding that, they began to work as professional songwriters in New York's celebrated Brill Building. This legendary musical address was once home to over a hundred and fifty writing teams, publishers, promoters, producers and management companies. It is located at 1619 Broadway, not far from Times Square, and was named after a haberdasher's emporium that sat at street level.

King has often described the conditions there as basic to say the least. As songwriters, they would be put in a small room, practically a cubicle, which was just big enough to hold a battered upright piano, a chair and maybe a little desk for the lyricist to work at. They would also hear rival composers knocking up their latest songs through the inadequately soundproofed walls. It was like living in a rundown housing project for pop composers of legendary genius. Some of the compositions they eavesdropped on would become some of the best loved songs in all the world. Other writers working there at one time or another included Burt Bacharach and Hal David, Bobby Darin, Jerry Leiber and Mike Stoller, Neil Diamond, Neil Sedaka, Tommy Boyce and Bobby Hart, David Gates, Laura Nyro, Ellie Greenwich and Jeff Barry, Doc Pomus and Mort Shuman, Sonny Bono, Paul Simon and Phil Spector. From those draughty cacophonous corridors crashed such songs as 'The Look of Love', 'Walk on By', 'Yakety Yak', 'Save the Last Dance for Me', 'Breaking Up is Hard to Do' and 'River Deep, Mountain High'.

Goffin and King themselves turned out a prodigious amount of material in those years, in an atmosphere that was highly competitive. If you knew Bobby Vee's producer was coming in the next day, you had to have songs ready for him to hear. How easily the words and music came is hard to know but come they did as just a small selection from Carole and Gerry's catalogue includes 'Halfway to Paradise', 'Take Good Care of My Baby', 'Up on the Roof', 'I'm Into Something Good', 'One Fine Day', 'Pleasant Valley Sunday', 'The Loco-Motion' (for their babysitter Little Eva) and, not least, 'You Make Me Feel (Like a Natural Woman)'. Not bad days at the office, were they? Astonishing to think that as those Brill Building habitués knocked off work and mingled with the countless tens of thousands of office drones on the city streets they had just composed some of the most famous songs in popular music. Songs that would be cherished and sung for all of time.

Perhaps less surprising is the male domination of the scene. There were women involved but they were all working with their husbands, with the exception of the mercurially talented and fragile Laura Nyro. Ellie Greenwich and Cynthia Weil were married to Jeff Barry and Barry Mann respectively. King herself has talked of what an anomaly she was, as a mother of two living in New Jersey who had a job. Sadly Goffin's superlative qualities as a wordsmith were not mirrored by his fidelity. King was once embroiled in finding a home for her serial philanderer husband's mistress and their daughter. Goffin and King divorced in 1968. It was time for a change.

And for King, leaving her Stepford Wife life behind and heading for Laurel Canyon as a divorced mother of two certainly represented a change. The sunshine and the seductive hippie vibe must have seemed a whole world away from the pressure-cooker atmosphere of the Brill Building. The move to LA represented an escape from the tyranny of that daily process and also of married life to Gerry. She was free. No longer surrounded by rivals competing for the attention of the producers and hitmakers she fell in with the likes of Joni Mitchell and James Taylor, who were only concerned with writing songs for themselves about what was on their minds. There was no formula to it. In a sense The Beatles and Bob Dylan had heralded a new era of artists composing their own material, and as a proven writer there was no reason why Carole King shouldn't join the club once she mastered writing the words. It's perhaps impossible to imagine how seductive the whole atmosphere of Laurel Canyon and the attitudes of its inhabitants must have seemed for a still relatively young woman escaping the only life and city she had known.

Her first solo record was called *Writer* and appeared in 1970 but it was with *Tapestry* the following year that she made the world take notice of her as a solo artist. It stayed at number one in the US album charts for fifteen weeks and made her a genuine, if reluctant star. Intriguingly, as well as a batch of classic new songs, including 'I Feel the Earth Move', 'So Far Away', 'Beautiful', 'You've Got a Friend' and the title track itself, she also reclaimed a couple of Goffin and King classics. The Shirelles' 'Will You Love Me Tomorrow' and Aretha's 'You Make Me Feel (Like a Natural Woman)' were reappraised in a time of sexual liberation and the availability of the contraceptive pill. It was as if the songs had taken on a whole other meaning and one can only imagine what Gerry Goffin thought of that.

This change and the resultant album actually marks a significant stopping-off point on our journey. We have reached another crucial intersection. And not just for Carole King, but for female musicians and the womens' movement in general: nowhere is this made clearer than on the cover. The photograph, taken at King's own home, pictures her without make-up, barefoot, hair frizzy and non-coiffured, working on a patchwork in the company of her cat Telemachus, named after a character from Homer's *Odyssey*. Here, it said, was a woman who had taken control of her life and would live it in exactly the way she saw fit. The idea that stylists would mould you and airbrush you for public consumption was gone. In Laurel Canyon it was de rigeur to be natural even on the covers of your records. Crosby, Stills and Nash just lounged on a battered sofa outside a weather-beaten wooden house for their 1969 eponymous debut album, although they didn't really think it through, possibly because a chemical roll-up had been inhaled. From left to right on the sleeve they were seated as Nash, Stills and Crosby, which confused everyone. Apparently, they did go back the next day to try and rectify the situation, only to find the well-used couch had been taken away. In a way, it's better as it is: it somehow just sums up the Laurel Canyon state of mind. Sit anywhere you like, lads, and we'll just take a couple of snaps. It was crucial not to appear to be trying too hard.

Tapestry became one of those albums that everyone had to have. Or certainly if you were a certain kind of young woman, you had to have it. Every girl I knew had it: that's three copies in Bolton alone. It not only expressed independence and liberation as big ideas and principles but also seemed to connect to the most intimate and personal feelings. It was having its cake and eating it, as was Carole in the blissed-out canyon. It's not a political record in the shadow of Vietnam, it isn't an album of Dylan-esque protest songs, but it does remind us that in times of great trial we sometimes have to find the strength from within. It is a record of truth. Of the deepest and most profound thoughts and of songs written not to order for the charts but to search for the answers within, somehow.

On 3 July 2016 the slight and slightly apologetic-looking, still frizzy-haired Carole King stepped out on to the stage at Hyde Park in London to perform the album in its entirety and in its original running order for the very first time to mark its forty-fifth anniversary. Sixty-five thousand people came to hear it. What a triumphant celebration of an album that not only transformed the life of its creator, but was such an inspiration to all those who bought it back in 1971.

21

Hail! Hail! Rock and Roll!

As we've been looking at some of the crucial turning points in the history of pop, it must therefore be self-evident that there can be few more important moments than the release of the first rock and roll record. 'Rocket "88"' by Jackie Brenston and his Delta Cats might sound a bit like a boogie-woogie record but it is generally accepted that it is the earliest to be classed as rock and roll, even if one of its architects, the talented if volatile, objectionable and contrary Ike Turner, didn't consider it to be part of the genre at all.

'Rocket "88"' was recorded at Sun Studios in Memphis, Tennessee, on either the 3rd or 5th of March in 1951, and so while we were on our tour of those parts, me and my travelling companions, Jamie and Phil, had to go down there and see where it all began.

On the Sunday we visited, it was bucketing down with rain in Memphis and dossing around in the lobby of our hotel waiting for a taxi – repeated calls to the office promised it was 'just around the corner' – our window of opportunity at Sun was ebbing away. How we could have done with the devilish driver of Chapter 1, who would have had us down there in a flash, before going on somewhere to get laid no doubt. Sadly neither he nor what looked increasingly like an entirely mythical cab that had been 'just around the corner' for about forty-five minutes turned up and so we decided to brave the elements, having been assured that our destination was only a short walk out of town.

This proved something of an understatement. Trudging an unremarkable boulevard for what seemed like miles – past truck rental depots, petrol stations and the odd donut store – in the lashing storm wasn't how I'd envisaged arriving at Sun Studios. At times it seemed impossible that we were on the right road so unprepossessing did it seem, but whenever we asked any of the few-and-far-between and similarly drenched passersby, we were assured that if we squelched a few blocks further down Union Avenue we would indeed eventually come to a crossroads and the all-important number 706.

Eventually, there it was, appearing like a mirage through the clouds of squall, with the neon S, U and N letters beckoning us the last few sodden yards. It's a small-ish two-storey building, with a large guitar hanging from the corner elevation with Marshall Avenue, and the studio itself's in a sort of one-floor annexe to the side. We slithered through the doorway into a diner-cum-record-store-cum-memorabilia outlet and, eternally grateful to have found shelter, began our exploration of this most historic shrine.

Radio man Sam Phillips opened the studio as the Memphis Recording Service on 3 January 1950 and paid one hundred and fifty dollars a month to rent the building. Into these humble halls would eventually wander legends like Johnny Cash, Jerry Lee Lewis, Roy Orbison, Carl Perkins, B.B. King, Howlin' Wolf and, one blisteringly hot day in 1953, the eighteen-year-old Elvis Presley – intent, apparently, on making an acetate recording as a gift for his mother. When asked by receptionist and loyal Phillips lieutenant Marion Keisker who he sounded like, the future superstar is reputed to have said, 'I don't sound like nobody.'

Sitting in that reception area with the original furniture still in situ – probably, sometimes it's best not to shatter your own illusions by asking too many questions – it seemed amazing to think that we were on the very spot where Elvis's career began. Incredible to ponder that that was the first time he would have walked through the doors of a recording studio, and to speculate on whether he would have walked all the way from town if it had been tipping it down, like it was the day we visited. That kind of downpour would surely have had catastrophic effects on the teenage quiff. Fate maybe. The sun shone on the King.

The recording room itself is perhaps thirty feet by twenty, and its walls and ceiling are lined with slightly irregularly applied perforated acoustic tiles. Some of these are reputed to be parts of the original fabric of the building and that's good enough for me. It could be rather like the Cavern in Liverpool, as we've already discussed vaguely – on the same site as the famous old club and reconstituted in part from the same bricks. Unlike the Cavern, though, there's no doubting that Sun is exactly where it always has been, and it is extraordinary to stand in a room where Elvis Presley recorded 'That's All Right Mama', Carl Perkins rattled through 'Blue Suede Shoes', Jerry Lee Lewis tore up 'Whole Lotta Shakin' Goin' On' and a young Johnny Cash laid down 'Folsom Prison Blues'. I guess you're either someone who really feels these things or you're not, but I definitely felt a quiver of excitement standing in that most sacred of places, and it wasn't just shivering with cold from being soaked to the skin.

There were even old microphones you could hold and sing into, that might, quite possibly, have been used by Presley himself. Imagine your hand where his had been. Maybe. Again, you can be the kind of person who wants cast-iron provenance or you just accept that the probability is thrill enough. He might have wrapped his hand around this artefact, and 'might' will do. If you visit a battlefield you don't get to handle the actual spears and arrows they winged at each other, do you? But it's still a thrill and a visceral experience to be on the spot where it happened. And that's what it's like being at Sun Studios. Those early proponents of rock and roll stood on this actual floor where your own liberally doused trainers are standing now and made pop history – and if you don't get a little thrill from that there's something wrong with you. Unless you're not interested in rock and roll at all, in which case what are you doing at Sun Studios, you idiot?

Naturally, if you want to feel really close to Elvis you go to Graceland, which is where we were taken by our Mephistopheles of the minicab from Chapter 1. You don't drive through the famous gates any more, but get dropped off in a kind of slightly soulless Presley mall, with numerous burger joints and rather characterless halls holding exhibitions of his cars and clothes and the like. I felt rather disappointed that you couldn't buy a gigantic, grease-laden baguette loaded with several pounds of bacon and a jar each of peanut butter and jelly; while you couldn't advocate his dietary habits it seems only fair that everyone should have the chance to live like a king for one day. Even if you feel dreadful the next. At least your temporary gluttony and distended belly would bring you closer to the spirit of the man, don't you think?

And so you are ferried by shuttle bus across a busy highway and up to the house itself, which is, by modern celebrity mansion standards, petite but still impressive with its 'Petit Trianon meets Colonial homestead' arrangement of pillars. The first rooms you see are a lounge and dining room, revealing a Rococo-Romany stylistic leaning and which initially seem quite garish, but will pale into insignificance when compared to the excesses to come. The oft-photographed pool-table room is swathed in multicoloured fabric on the walls and the ceiling with an Art Deco-style lamp suspended over the baize. There are sofas around the walls and no windows. It's hard not to imagine that when it was occupied by Elvis and a fistful of burly henchmen from the Memphis Mafia smoking cigars and eating deep-fried cottage loaves it must have been a claustrophobic and oppressive place to be. It must have been very easy, when drawing back a cue, to poke someone in the eye and put them right off their five thousand calorie late-night amuse-bouche.

Similarly, a basement den where bright yellow leather has been selected as the cornerstone of the design concept seems unnecessarily cramped. It's underground, so again there is no natural light. There are three television sets set into a mirrored wall, a small banana-coloured bar and a three-sided sofa in the middle of which, on a glass-topped coffee table, sits a statuette of a bemused monkey, looking like a Roswell alien and casting an imperious gaze on the room. What sights has that little fella seen over the years, eh? Well, none, as he is ceramic, but the room looks like a Seventies Maltese business-man's idea of a discotheque. The jungle room does at least have natural light but is carpeted in what appears to be fake grass and festooned with oversized ethnic wooden carvings. A waterfall used to run down one stone wall, though sadly no longer. Apparently Priscilla Presley used to enjoy relaxing here – and no wonder. Every other room was filled with ageing Teddy Boys farting, smoking, pushing their cholesterol levels ever higher and laughing at Elvis's jokes.

And then there's the kitchen from where his private

twenty-four-hour snacketeria operated. Again, it's not huge but with its dark wood units, hints of orange and heavily patterned carpet feels slightly like it's closing in on you. What a very strange place it must have been as the King's court of friends and family members adapted their lifestyles and timetables to their lord and master's every whim. They were all on the payroll: what Elvis said went.

It's very easy to scoff and to forget how things came to this. Elvis was a hillbilly from a shotgun shack in Tupelo, another indelible sight we took in on our road trip. He had no middle-class interior design sensibilities. He let his imagination run riot with the house and yet my lasting memory of Graceland was of a peaceful place. At the back of the house are stables and acres of undulating farmland, crisscrossed with picket fences, and you begin to see that what Presley was doing was creating a little world where he could live freely with his mates and the people who mattered to him and ride horses, race go-karts or play racquet ball away from the prying eyes of his adoring public. He wasn't free once he went outside those wrought iron gates but once secured in the compound he could let his guard down. It was all really rather sweet and made you feel a great deal of affection for someone who seemed like a friendly, generous and decent guy.

Intriguingly, you are not allowed upstairs at Graceland. You pass the bottom of the staircase, knowing full well that up there is the imperial bedroom and the lavishly appointed en suite where he met his end, and it's hard not to let your imagination run riot: it is rumoured to have remained unchanged since that fateful August night in 1977. In fact, there are those who insist that it remains so unchanged that Elvis is alive and well and lives up there still, marooned in his chamber, watching the worshipping hordes through net curtains. Though one has to bear in mind that people who think that are fools who don't think Neil Armstrong and Buzz Aldrin walked on the moon.

So what would be terrific now is to tell you how Elvis went into Sun Studios and made the very first rock and roll record. Unfortunately, I can't do that as he was beaten to that honour by a good three years by the aforementioned 'Rocket "88"' by Jackie Brenston and his Delta Cats. You might well never have heard of Jackie Brenston, who was a sax player and vocalist who later became an alcoholic truck driver – never a good combination. However, the group were actually the Kings of Rhythm under another name, and were led by the ever-charming Clarksdale-born bandleader and wife-beater Ike Turner who took Tina to a live sex show in a brothel in Tijuana on their wedding night. What a guy.

One of the most noted aspects of 'Rocket "88"' has been its claim to feature distorted guitar for the first time. It was played by Willie Kizart and there are several versions of how the sound was happened upon. All involve accounts of mishaps on the way to the recording – believeable since bands often travel to engagements in overcrowded and barely roadworthy vehicles. I shudder now at the thought of going from Manchester to do a gig in Sheffield with a band I was in, over the tortuous and copiously iced Snake Pass. There were five of us – so not a perfect pop group (in any way) – plus five members of the support band and a whole back line of amplification and two drum kits in that rusting box van, which looked like it had been around since rationing. We were also accompanied by a full PA system and three operatives in another clapped-out conveyance which duly conked out somewhere near the Ladybower Reservoir. Cheerfully unconcerned, we merely unloaded all the equipment out of their van and put it and them into our own already seriously overloaded crate and merrily went on our way, swinging round the hairpin bends with thirteen people and all that gear onboard with a bogbrush-headed punk rocker called Gus Gangrene at the wheel. I mean, what could possibly go wrong? I suppose it could have been worse: on another occasion my mate said he would get a van from his dad's work to convey us to the poorly attended and ill-received concert and when it came it was a pick-up truck, meaning that three of us had to travel in the open air with the equipment. And this in February.

Poor Willie Kizart, whose amplifier probably cost him six months' pay on the plantation, loaded his precious cargo onto the roof rack of the car and legend has it that it later fell off somewhere on Highway 61. The movements of impoverished musicians are fraught with problems. I'd like to tell you it happened at the crossroads with Highway 49 and that Satanic forces were involved but I can't be that specific. Ike Turner, the reliability of whose word is questionable, always reckoned that the amp had been stored in the trunk but had been subject to rainwater damage causing the sonic collywobbles. A third version has the automobile getting a flat tyre and the equipment being dropped onto the roadway while the assembled cats of the Delta retrieved the spare from the bottom of the boot. Whichever way it happened, though, the amp sounded terrible when they plugged it in at Sun. In my day, we'd have searched out a tube of Copydex latex glue to line the speaker cone in an attempt to eradicate the aural flatulence. For some reason Sam Phillips thought it might help if they stuffed the amplifier with screwed-up newspapers. This would likely exacerbate the problem in my view but, evidently happy with the resulting noise, they went ahead and laid down the track, thus creating the birth of rock and roll on record. Like so many significant musical moments it was a happy accident though how happy Willie Kizart was to have a knackered amp padded out with copies of the *Memphis Bugle*, or whatever the local rag was called, is not on record.

What is for sure is that one of the signature sounds of rock and roll was, inadvertently, invented here in the distorted guitar. Think of such disparate classics as Black Sabbath's 'Paranoid', The Troggs' 'Wild Thing', Steppenwolf's 'Born to Be Wild', Python Lee Jackson's 'In a Broken Dream', Nirvana's 'Smells Like Teen Spirit' and even the sublime 'Have You Seen Her?' by The Chi-Lites, and then reimagine them with pristine, non-distorted guitars. So much would have been lost.

Despite Willie Kizart's unexpected contribution to the story of rock, there are those who claim that the fuzzed guitar was first used by Dave Davies on The Kinks' 'You Really Got Me' in 1964. Davies has said that the sound was due to a fit of pique he had after splitting up with a girlfriend and taking a razor blade to the speaker cone in his amplifier. This may well be true, although it seems an awfully strange thing to do. For a start you are sabotaging the tools of your trade, but also it would seem to be a very precise operation to undertake while soundly miffed. You've also got to go to the trouble of finding a razor blade and then, having done so, go into the back of the amp to attack the cone. It's going to quite a lot of trouble, as opposed to just dinging the guitar on the corner of the cabinet or flinging a teacup across the room. Nevertheless, the explanation for the influential sound on that record comes from Dave himself and so that peculiar reaction to being jilted resulted in one of the signature sounds in rock and roll and led to the invention of the fuzzbox.

Incidentally the 'Rocket "88"' is a very cool-looking car made by Oldsmobile and the Americans have always had a knack of making and naming cars that slot right into rock and roll. We didn't have that gift in the UK at that time. No one immortalised the Triumph Herald, Ford Prefect or Austin A40 Somerset with a wild distorted guitar, did they?

22

The Open Road

How extraordinary must the success of Kraftwerk's *Autobahn* have seemed on its release in 1974. Other huge albums that year were *Pretzel Logic* by Steely Dan, *What Were Once Vices Are Now Habits* by The Doobie Brothers, *On the Border* by the Eagles, *On the Beach* by Neil Young, John Lennon's *Walls and Bridges*, *Dark Horse* by Lennon's erstwhile bandmate George Harrison, *Queen II* and *Waterloo* by ABBA. Admittedly, *Meet the Residents* by The Residents, those shadowy, massive eyeball-headed Louisiana avant-garde pranketeers, also saw the light of the day, but if the bulk of that list gives you some idea of public taste at the time, then how on earth could the *Autobahn* LP, with side one devoted to twenty-two minutes and forty-three seconds of the title track, climb to number four in the UK album charts and number five in the States?

The edited single version became a global hit as the hypnotic ticking rhythm and Doppler effect parping car horns became a fixture on radios all over the world. Sure, the main sung refrain bore a passing resemblance to 'Barbara Ann' by The Beach Boys, whose *Endless Summer* compilation also came out in 1974, but there had to be more to it than that. Kraftwerk had come up with a masterplan at a crossroads where they left all acoustic instruments behind and headed off down the electrical freeway to unlikely international stardom.

The two figures at the centre of the Kraftwerk story, the twin colossi if you like, are Ralf Hütter and Florian Schneider. They met as students in the late Sixties when Florian was studying flute and violin and Ralf organ and piano. It seems that they were very much influenced by an exhibition of the art of Gilbert and George and the representation of two men, handsomely besuited, largely expressionless, but seemingly joined at the hip. This is an image Gilbert and George have maintained right up to the present day. Always together, ever-eccentric creatures of habit dining at the same café at the same time every day, immaculately turned out and hugely successful. Life becomes part of the art – and certainly Kraftwerk admired that aesthetic.

The band formed in Düsseldorf in 1970, and their early albums show a search for a signature sound as they tumble through elements of free jazz and art rock. Other musicians like drummer Klaus Dinger and guitarist Michael Rother, who went on to found the hugely influential NEU!, came and went. Florian was still tootling around on the flute and Ralf even had long hair – albeit in a peculiar side-parted style with mulletish fronds cascading to the rear. Never a good look. It was almost like he was wearing two haircuts at the same time, and the only person who's ever pulled that off successfully is Phil Oakey in the early days of The Human League, one of the legions of bands who owe Kraftwerk a colossal debt of gratitude.

In 1973 Kraftwerk released the *Ralf and Florian* album, cementing their position as electronic music's Gilbert and George, if not yet with the knack of writing catchy tunes like Gilbert and Sullivan. The rear cover shows the two of them sitting in a chilly-looking room with bare brick walls painted gallery white. They are in a sense their own installation. Florian still has a few wind instruments around him but you can really feel the largely instrumental tracks edging towards the classic Kraftwerk blueprint that would conquer the world the following year. They've also had little neon signs made of their names which they've placed on the floor in front of them, which again shows an artsy playfulness. Perhaps the intense effort in presenting the group as a two-headed beast is why the absence of Florian from the ranks since 2008 has felt so painful. Even if it wasn't always clear what, if anything, he was doing we just wanted him to be there bookending Ralf at the other side of the stage.

The idea for 'Autobahn' is simple enough: a Toad from *The Wind in the Willows*-like love of the open road. As is well documented, the members of Kraftwerk's first love was the bicycle and not the car. I was lucky enough, while working at Piccadilly Radio, to meet the band on

their 1981 'Computer World' tour, seeing them at
Manchester's Free Trade Hall, the Royal Court Theatre
in Liverpool and the Lyceum in London. After flying
into Manchester they unloaded their bikes at the airport
and cycled into town, or at least Ralf and Florian did.
I'm not sure percussionists Karl Bartos and Wolfgang
Flür, by then the other members of the expanded four-
piece line-up, embraced pedal power quite so
enthusiastically.

I remember vividly going to the concert in Manchester,
which was followed by a record company-funded Italian
meal at Cesare's in the company of Ralf and Wolfgang,
and then bumping into Florian the following morning
in Piccadilly Gardens. Evidently suffering from some
joint trouble and possibly saddle rash, if that's a thing,
he politely explained to me all the various unguents he
had bought from Boots that morning, drawing each one
out of the small carrier bag by way of illustration. How
surreal was that? You meet one of your musical heroes
one-to-one and he is talking about bollock balm. But
Ralf and Florian were very serious about their cycling.
In fact the other members of the team often expressed
frustration that they could have got more music done
if their colleagues hadn't been swathed in Lycra and
holding up irate motorists on the back lanes of North
Rhine-Westphalia. Work on recording stopped completely
in 1983 when Hütter had a serious cycling accident,
which left him temporarily in a coma. Hütter and
Schneider always prided themselves on a stern work
ethic, professing to clock in for a very un-rock-and-roll

nine-to-five working day at their Kling Klang studio, where they refused to install a phone to avoid unnecessary interruptions.

You can't ride your bike on the autobahn of course so the members of Kraftwerk must have resorted to cars at certain times. I don't know which models they would have driven but I like to think of them in something small and vaguely comic like a DAF. The artwork for the record features a rather stately-looking black Mercedes sedan and a classic Volkswagen Beetle, but neither seems quite right for our boys. I just like the idea of them pootling around in underpowered fart-boxes on roads with no speed limit and so, when interviewing Wolfgang Flür, I was delighted to hear that he sometimes sees Florian 'and I wave to him in his little car. With my hand.'

The idea for the autobahn network first came in the Twenties at the time of the Weimar Republic, but not much progress was made due to the hyperinflation that had resulted from First World War reparation payments; this led to banknotes being worth so little there are photographs of children in the streets using bundles of them as make-shift building-block toys. In 1922 a loaf of bread cost one hundred and sixty marks. A year later it was two hundred thousand million marks. No, really. With that in mind, it's easy to understand why the motorway plan was put on hold for a while. It was the rise of the Nazis that accelerated the programme; Hitler was determined to build a motorised society and in fact the VW Beetle was the result of his instruction to create a people's car. Into the Forties and such was the level of car production that a whole new city called Wolfsburg was built to house the workforce for the gigantic car plants. In a way, the new industrial revolution and development would come to inspire auto- mated musical innovation in the music of Kraftwerk and others who came in their wake.

The first crossroads-free route for vehicles ran between Bonn and Cologne and opened in 1932 with a speed limit of seventy-five miles per hour. Given that the average car of those times – an Opel Olympia or Skoda Superb, say – struggled to reach a top speed of fifty comfortably that seems inordinately high. I'm reliably informed that if you had a nine-and-a-half litre Hispano-Suiza J12 you might easily top that figure but not many people had that much cash to blow on a car. The first section of autobahn ran between Frankfurt and Darmstadt and opened in 1935. There was no speed limit, which remains the case to this day, except for certain zones. By 1936 one hundred and thirty thousand people were working on what was to become the first high-speed road network in the world. It was a major achievement, even if its completion will be forever rooted in Nazi history. Being born just after the Second World War it's clear that, being all too well aware of their country's recent past, Hütter and Schneider must have been easily seduced by the notion of the relatively new-found freedom that the autobahn not only offered practically, but also symbol- ised in a wider sense. Perhaps new fans internationally bought into that notion too, as the single hit the UK charts at number eleven and twenty-five in the US.

But primarily, it was a hit because it was great pop

music. Just great pop music that had been produced in a different way than anyone had tried before. Yes, it is electronic; yes, it contains ambient recordings; yes, it is conceptual art, but first and foremost it is a catchy pop tune. And Kraftwerk have always understood what being a pop group entailed. The *Autobahn* album sees the arrival of Wolfgang Flür on electronic percussion, but the true classic period of the band begins on the next record, *Radioactivity*, which is unveiled in 1975. A further percussionist has been enlisted in Karl Bartos and now the iconic four-piece is in place. The electronic Beatles have been created.

As we discussed in relation to the Ramones, four is the perfect number for a pop group. During the 2010 UK General Election campaign a televised debate took place between Gordon Brown, Nick Clegg and David Cameron. Each was placed behind a lectern, prompting larky headlines of 'worst Kraftwerk gig ever'. When this was put to Ralf Hütter he dismissed the comparison, saying, 'because there's only three of them. One is missing.' Bang on, Ralf. It has to be four. If you see Kraftwerk now there are indeed four of them in a line behind consoles. They don't appear to be doing all that much but it's very difficult to tell. That's the nature of electronic music. It is machine-driven; you can't expect to see lots of physical histrionics going on. If you tour a nuclear power station you don't want to see lots of blokes running around sweating with lump hammers and wrenches, do you? You want a sense of calm with a few white-coated spods pressing the odd button and monitoring computer displays with a sage nod. Similarly, if you go and watch Kraftwerk, you don't want Ralf to leave his podium and do some dad dancing with a bit of air guitar thrown in. And no one wants to see a keyboard player overdoing the gurning, do they? Rock posturing for a lead guitarist or vocalist is par for the course and can be got away with as long as you're thin with good hair. But an overly effervescent keyboard player is just wrong. It is a sedentary job and should be accepted as such and the mentalist who invented the 'key-tar' should be forever subjected to ridicule and derision.

But there are four Kraftwerkers on stage and from what you can see it does seem to break down into more of a standard band line-up than you'd think. Ralf is on the far left and handles the vocals and the lead melodies. Next to him is Henning, the bald one, who is responsible for the bass parts. Moving to third left is Fritz, who bears an uncanny resemblance to my accountant Charles, and such is his level of concentration coupled with physical inactivity he could well be completing a tax return up there. But Fritz is in charge of percussion and beats. On the far right is where Florian should be but there we find Falk who is evidently controlling the visuals and projections. Okay, so that's not a standard job in a band – though when The Human League started they did have a member called Adrian Wright whose job was to display slides on the back of the stage. But the other three are basically a digital Emerson, Lake & Palmer.

Like all classic line-ups of classic bands, they eventually

split. Flür and Bartos, frustrated at the lack of progress with new music, left to undertake their own projects which have been moderately successful, if intermittent. I have interviewed both of them in recent years and can report that they are quite the opposite of the stern Kraftwerk image. Bartos smiles from ear to ear all the time and bristles with energy and enthusiasm, and while he was in our radio studio animatedly conducted his own piece 'Atomium', named after the modernist sculptural reminder of the 1958 World Expo in Brussels, as it blasted out across the airwaves. He has also collaborated with Electronic and Pet Shop Boys, who are splendid fellows all, and so that's recommendation enough. Flür is less effusive, but very charming and extremely dry. Not to mention strikingly handsome. No wonder – as documented in his excellent memoir *I Was a Robot*, he decided in his wilder days to behave like a young man on a rock and roll tour rather than as an austere automaton. The book contains photographs that display his impish sense of humour as the famed Kraftwerk doppelgänger robots snog and goose each other backstage. To the evident chagrin of Hütter, Wolfgang was famous, desirable and away on tour, and was determined to make the most of the opportunities that came his way.

Kraftwerk as a brand continue to travel the world with their spectacular 3-D graphics and Ralf stands far left, calmly intoning the songs and leading the music that changed the face of pop music and reset notions of what a rock band could be.

Of Florian Schneider, nothing is heard. We have no

choice but to accept his retirement from public life and so he is, to me, forever frozen, rummaging in a carrier bag on Piccadilly Gardens before retiring to his hotel to lavishly anoint his nether regions with Deep Heat.

23

Background Music

**What do you call someone who
hangs around with musicians?**

A drummer.

As a provider of beats myself, I've had to put up
with these oft-repeated drummer jokes since I was
a pimply adolescent. How do you know when the drum
riser is straight? Because drool comes out of both sides
of the drummer's mouth. Hilarious. What's the difference
between a drummer and a drum machine? With a drum
machine you only have to punch the instructions in once.
Oh, my aching sides.

However, I have always taken solace from the other
accepted answer to the first question posed here. What
do you call someone who hangs around with musicians?
Brian Peter George St John le Baptiste de la Salle Eno.

For a start Brian Eno was a member of a massively successful and hugely influential band in Roxy Music for whom he operated a complicated-looking synthesizer with a large jack field, from which it looked feasible he was directing international trunk calls, albeit in rather glamorous attire. However, one of the key elements of Brian's performance was that he was manipulating the synth with a joystick rather than a keyboard. This meant that his contribution to the sound was a series of unpredictable and, one assumes, unrepeatable wheezes, farts, squeals and arpeggios which seasoned the sonic soup.

Now, you could take the view that this was tantamount to being part of the band while not actually doing very much, but this would be a controversial standpoint in my view. You could say that Bez didn't do anything in Happy Mondays except wander around idly gesticulating with the maracas and making his limbs go in four different directions simultaneously. But he was in a sense the 'vibemaster'. His being lost in a trance in their music made the whole thing more compelling somehow. Arrested Development had Baba Oje who was credited as 'spiritual advisor', which seemed to be nice work if you could get it; The Brian Jonestown Massacre included a 'spokesman of the revolution' called Joel Gion, whose duties seemed to be mainly tambourine-based. The Polyphonic Spree were a white-smocked commune of a band who appeared to have at least a dozen people doing next to nothing, which looked like an expensive way to operate, but it did make them quite fascinating in a weird religious cult kind of way.

But Eno's aural abstractions were a vital part of the Roxy Music melange. They already had guitar, bass, drums, keyboards, saxophone and oboe. They didn't need another melody instrument. They needed something that would make Bryan Ferry's brilliant, angular, off-kilter rock and roll songs sound like they might have been recorded on another planet. They needed treatments that would give them an eerie, otherworldly lustre and Eno provided this beautifully, even if, by his own admission, he wasn't always sure what he was doing.

Yet for the non-musician, not being sure what you are doing is a key part of the process. You have no musical ability or theory to fall back on and so you have no choice but to follow the paths that chance leads you down. To this end, Eno, who himself had spent plenty of time dossing around studying painting and experimental music at Ipswich Civic College and Winchester School of Art, collaborated with the multimedia artist and Sixties art school guru Peter Schmidt on the *Oblique Strategies* series of cards. As we established earlier, these are intended to encourage free thinking, often at the point of creative impasse, and selecting a few at random from my own personal set – while in no way suggesting that I am suffering from writer's block here – I find the following utterances:

'What to increase? What to reduce?'

'Don't be afraid of things because they're easy to do'

'Simply a matter of work'

and

'Once the search is in progress, something will
be found'

This is, of course, true of most creative endeavours. Not
everything starts with the luxury of a solid plan.
Sometimes there is a blank tape, page, canvas or stage
and you just have to start something without knowing
where it is going to lead you. Presumably this happened
to Brian every time he patched the spaghetti wires across
his synthesizer.

Perhaps the most famous and significant of the cards,
though, and again it came into play when discussing The
Beatles, reads as follows – as you'll no doubt recall:

'Honour thy error as a hidden intention'

Once you consider this premise it is a fantastically liber-
ating thought. Every alarming burp and screech that Eno
produced for Roxy he could quite safely say he meant,
even if he wasn't entirely sure how he'd done it. And it
is in some way this maxim that led to him going on to
produce such acts as Devo, Robert Wyatt, Genesis and
James, being a key collaborator with David Byrne and
Talking Heads, and also overseeing albums by probably
the biggest band in the world, U2. Of course, a producer
does not have to be a musician. He or she has to be an

enabler, someone who creates an atmosphere in which creativity can thrive, and often, with successful acts working to a tried and tested plan, this can involve encouraging them to take different processes and explore new patterns of operating.

Manchester band James have talked about Eno coming to the studio and setting up tables full of myriad electronic gadgets and processors, just to see what sounds would come out of the other end, in the hope of ending up somewhere you would never have got to if using your usual methods. And this sort of restless and enquiring mind has led to him being in demand with large companies and corporations to encourage what I suppose you'd call, in a now-detested splurge of management speak, 'blue sky thinking'. But once you embrace the idea that 'this is what we do, so what happens if we don't', you can see how it becomes creatively electrifying. You have no idea where you are going but 'once the search is in progress, something will be found'. And when you think about it, how many instances in our lives have been examples of this? How many of us have fallen in love with people we met randomly at some event we didn't really want to attend? The 'sliding doors' concept is concerned with how different our lives could have been if random sequences of events had somehow occurred differently, and if we appreciate this in life, then it seems only natural to apply it to the production of art. It must also follow that, with this in mind, if life imitates art and vice versa there has to be a point you can reach where the two intersect and it is precisely at one of these crossroads that Brian Eno invented ambient music. Well, maybe.

You can make a case for the genre having been created by Erik Satie, who could just possibly have pipped Eno to it by about sixty years. Satie was born in Honfleur, France in 1866. He was by no means a non-musician, entering the Paris Conservatoire in 1879. However, once there his piano playing was described by one of his tutors as 'insignificant and laborious'. Despite that, he became a prolific composer of not only the *Gymnopédies* and *Gnossiennes*, that are cherished and often heard to this day, but also a fantastic range of works including pieces for children and cabaret songs. Perhaps tired of the formal training, or possibly propelled by less than sympathetic teaching, Satie became a fixture of the Parisian avant-garde and was much taken with the principles of Dadaism.

One of his more out-there projects was something called *Musique d'Ameublement,* which he composed in 1917. Translated as 'Furniture Music', these were five short pieces to be played at various soirées but, in his own words, to 'mingle with the sound of knives and forks at dinner'. Quite how practical this was, with live ensembles of musicians in the room, is hard to assess – there was only one recorded performance in Satie's lifetime so if there were issues, they probably never got ironed out. The instructions for the recital of the works specify unlimited repeats and it has been said that Satie's ideas directly influenced the American minimalist composers for whom repetition became a key notion:

La Monte Young, Terry Riley, Philip Glass, Steve Reich and certainly John Cage, who later arranged a performance of 'Furniture Music'.

But the concept here is fascinating. Often the term 'background music' is intended as dismissive. It implies the work is so bland and inoffensive that it doesn't hold the attention, instead just becoming a sort of aural wallpaper. But what if – and we're back to considering strategies of the oblique variety here – we take that as a positive rather than a negative? What if music that Satie said was 'not imposing itself' became part of the environment and not something that dominated?

We've all experienced music like this. I remember vividly as a nine-year-old in 1967 hearing radios through open windows playing psychedelic records like Traffic's 'Hole in My Shoe' and 'Kites' by Simon Dupree and the Big Sound. Both are ethereal-sounding tracks and feature enigmatic spoken-word sections which seem to suggest a portal to another mind-altered world. This could probably be achieved only with the aid of LSD but of course as I was still in single figures I couldn't be expected to know any of that. And yet the mysterious sounds somehow mingled with the general background hubbub of Bolton life to create an intoxicating blend I can recall even now. Perhaps you've heard a distant brass band in a parade or at a bandstand across the park. Maybe you've heard the throb of a party sound system across your back garden. At a festival you might well stray into the hinterland between two stages and inadvertently create dissonance in your ears until you move on. Every time you listen to music in the car you will have experienced something like this, unless you are one of those pin-headed, acnefied baseball-capped no-marks who plays their grime music so loud it seems like it might threaten the structural integrity of their 03-plate Vauxhall Corsa. So ambient music, music that is part of our environment, has always existed.

The idea of background music being part of everyday life took an interesting twist in 1954 when the concept of Muzak was trademarked. Initially intended as a way of transmitting music down wires rather than by radio waves to expensive and unreliable receivers, it gradually became known as 'elevator' or 'lift music' and was a bland and sanitising presence in many public spaces. No shopping mall was complete without the wafting clouds of unthreatening Muzak melodies. Eventually it was bought by Warner Bros and became something of a global curse. Sinister theories emerged of music being processed into fifteen-minute blocks where the tempo indiscernibly increased to improve productivity when piped into the workplace. Custom-made playlists were designed for specific customers, which anticipates some bespoke streaming services, in a way. Eventually, original songs began to appear as part of the mix as well as the anodyne light orchestral pieces and Muzak became a catch-all term for innocuous background music. It became recognised as something of an invasive plague and at one point loincloth-sporting Republican and grizzled hunting, shooting, fishing wild man of the fuzz guitar Ted Nugent was reported to be considering a ten-million dollar bid for the company just so he could shut it down. So although Muzak could be considered as ambient music in that it was created to contribute to the surroundings we found ourselves in, it was too strident and insistent to form part of a mix of sounds. It was overly dominant in all its installations and therefore can't be considered as ambient music in the true sense.

If we happily dismiss Muzak, and more reluctantly Erik Satie, we can say that Eno invented ambient music, right? I think so, although in 1964 the American jazz clarinetist Tony Scott released an album called *Music for Zen Meditation*. This is generally considered to be the first 'new age' record. New age music is calming and predominantly instrumental material which is supposed to aid a sense of wellbeing and spiritual enlightenment, though can just as often be found swirling through garden centres while you decide which bird feeder to buy. Scott followed it up with *Music for Yoga Meditation and Other Joys* in 1968. Another LP from 1964, entitled *Soothing Sounds for Baby* – and you can probably work out for yourself what that was all about – was bizarrely created by an American composer and inventor called Raymond Scott, whose works also feature in many Looney Tunes and Merrie Melodies cartoons and are some of the least ambient pieces of music you will ever hear. New age material is, though, more reliant on formal melody and structure than true ambient music and so finally we get to Brian Eno as he reaches a moment of musical revelation.

Unfortunately, Eno's inspiration only came about

following a car accident. Again, it is an example of how a random event led to a discovery that would perhaps otherwise have remained unmade. Recovering in bed and unable to move, Eno was bidding goodbye to a visitor who asked if he wanted any music on before she left. He replied in the affirmative and so an album of eighteenth-century harp music was placed on the turntable. However, the volume was set very low and one of the speakers of the stereo system wasn't working anyway. To compound the situation, it was raining heavily, and so the sound of the drops falling onto the roof also conspired to partially obliterate the angelic plucking. Bedbound Bri was not able to get up to wiggle the connections and whack the volume up, so he just lay there listening to a combination of faint glissandos and pitter-pattering precipitation. Gradually, though, frustration gave way to fascination as he revisited Satie's notion of music that doesn't impose itself. Music that becomes a sort of sonic interior design would later be central to his sound installations in public spaces across the world. It wasn't Muzak. It didn't dominate. It could blend with the natural sounds of birdsong, wind, rain, footsteps, chatter, echoey Tannoy announcements and the clatter of crockery, and indeed with the light and space, to form part of a complete environment.

'Discreet Music' was Eno's first work directly exploring these ideas. Thirty minutes long, and included on his album of the same name, it consists of slowly moving synthesizer figures delayed and replayed over each other to create an effect rather like a wave gently washing over you.

In a way it's tempting to look at what was going on in the world in general to see if ambient music was a response to events that were taking place in 1975. Eno was a techno-freak and it was certainly a year of technological advance with JVC introducing VHS and Sony the doomed Betamax. Margaret Thatcher became leader of the opposition, for the Conservative Party, and Britain was engaged in the Cod Wars with Iceland. Were we looking for a calming soundtrack to escape the sense of unrest and upheaval? Or as the Vietnam War finally ended with the fall of Saigon, were we in need of post-traumatic soothing? Intriguingly, this was also the year when Britain voted to join the Common Market (Brex-in?), and so perhaps we needed time to reflect on that. In a way, the *Discreet Music* album offers the polar opposite of another landmark album released this same year: Bruce Springsteen's *Born to Run*.

Okay, these may all be far-fetched thoughts but ambient music remains a brilliant concept. In fact, the word ambient has been widely adopted since Eno's early experiments. Aphex Twin released *Selected Ambient Works* in the early 1990s and bands like Autechre, The Orb, Boards of Canada and The KLF have ventured into the territory with countless others. There is also ambient dub, ambient techno and ambient house. There is even the ambient sausage roll though that turns out to be a less interesting phenomenon than it first seems.

As I listen to 'Discreet Music' now, on a spring-like

day in February with the window open to the birds singing and next door's dog Cassie barking, it works perfectly, though I do perhaps find myself listening more closely than was Brian's intention. Hang on, I'll turn it down a bit. Yes, that's better. I can hear the sound of a plane far and high away in the blue sky now. And a distant strimmer. The mix is complete.

24

The Red, White and Blue

I magine, if you can, being the best person in the world at something. How must that feel? How many people will ever know how that feels? A few sports stars, I guess, who have results and statistics to back them up. Lionel Messi might have an inkling. Perhaps if you are the richest person in the world or a given country you are, by definition, the best at making money. I think I am the best in the world at doing my radio show as it is what I say it is and though you are quite welcome, and some may say well advised, not to like it, I am still the best in the world at it because I have set the rules. Although to be fair, it is a bit rubbish some days. I keep trying though and have been doing for forty years now. They can always get someone else to do it, but then it ceases to be my radio show and therefore I'm still the best because without me it doesn't exist. Someone else quite possibly will be better, but that doesn't change the fact that I was best at doing it my way.

Beyond that, all judgements on being the best – and certainly in the arts – are deeply subjective. No one can say who the greatest artist or writer in the world is or was. You can have your favourites but other people will have different favourites to yours; that doesn't make them wrong. Unless they say the best writer in the world is Jackie Collins. Although she has sold loads more books than me, so perhaps I should avoid taking such cheap shots. Then again, if I'd avoided taking cheap shots this book would have finished many pages ago and who's to say that would have been a bad thing? You might also think of this as a pointless digression but you should be used to that by now and anyway this bit may well get scrapped by my editor. Let's wait and see, shall we?

In terms of the creation of art you can't say that anyone is definitively the best. Except Jimi Hendrix. Jimi Hendrix is the best player of the electric lead guitar that has ever lived. The Rock and Roll Hall of Fame has dubbed him 'the greatest instrumentalist in the history of rock music'. He had everything. He looked great, dressed fabulously at all times, had worked in many road bands to sharpen his chops and had the ability to use the Stratocaster as a sonic portal into worlds that were yet to be explored. He's not alone in this sense. Other guitar sounds have the ability to transport you to a certain time and place. The wah-wah guitar on Isaac Hayes' 1971 'Theme from Shaft' takes you directly to the ghetto. Keith Richards' fuzztone lead line which opens '(I Can't Get No) Satisfaction' places you on Carnaby Street at the height of swinging London. Pete

Townshend's feedback and crackling pick-up deselection on 'My Generation' instantly recalls the rebellious feelings of disenchanted youth. Perhaps most potently of all, just a few of the cascading notes from Roger McGuinn's Rickenbacker twelve-string at the start of 'Mr Tambourine Man' by The Byrds, and you can feel what it must have been like to be lozzing around in the sunshine in San Francisco with a herbal cheroot in your hand waiting for the Summer of Love to get underway. All these sounds are as vivid a snapshot of their times as any photograph, but none of the players had the charisma and almost alchemical power of Hendrix. If they had, they wouldn't have queued round the block to see him.

In 1967 Hendrix played at the world-famous Marquee Club on London's Wardour Street. Some say he played three gigs, others insist it was four. The confusion may arise from the fact that we have the dates for three concerts, but there was also a recording filmed there for the German TV programme *Beat Club*. What is known is that the guest list for the gig Hendrix played on 24 January included The Beatles, the Rolling Stones, Eric Clapton and Jeff Beck. Five days later, when he played again, Pete Townshend and Jimmy Page had also been added to the list. And it wasn't just the rock aristocracy who were drawn to see this shaman in action. It is said that over his three Marquee shows he played to fourteen hundred people and at one time the queue stretched along Wardour Street onto Shaftesbury Avenue and down towards Cambridge Circus. The legend had already been created. In fact, the buzz began even before he took the stage. Chas Chandler, bassist for The Animals and future Hendrix manager, had been so impressed with seeing Jimi in New York that he flew him over to London.

Hendrix's first full day in England was 22 September 1966. On that day he and Chandler went down to the music shops on Denmark Street where Hendrix duly tried out a few guitars to the general open-mouthed amazement of the assembled staff and customers. When Chandler ran into a friend called Mick Eve, who was saxophonist for Georgie Fame and the Blue Flames, he invited him inside to hear his new protégé. Eve apparently said he didn't need to go into the shop as he could hear a genius was at work from the pavement outside. In a way it seemed inevitable that, though Jimi was relatively unknown in his own country at this point, he would become an instant megastar; just as well, since sadly he wasn't going to be around all that long. Amazing to think that someone who left such an indelible impression had a mainstream career that lasted just four years.

Hendrix was born in Seattle in 1942 and his ascent as a guitarist began after he left the army. After getting into some bother with the law over riding in stolen cars, he was given the choice of prison or the armed forces. Not unreasonably he chose the latter and so found himself at Fort Campbell, Kentucky, as a reluctant recruit of the 101st Airborne Division where he met bassist Billy Cox, who would later stand alongside Hendrix on the stage at Woodstock on that historic day. With Mitch Mitchell, Noel Redding and Buddy Miles all gone now,

Cox is pretty much the last recognised Hendrix sideman still alive to tell the tales.

Perhaps unsurprisingly Jimi seems to have been a less than perfect squaddie. He was found asleep on duty, was a poor marksman and missed several midnight bed checks, which perhaps points to the nocturnal lifestyle so beloved of the committed rock star. My preferred time for a gig to finish is around nine in the evening but for those crazy cats the night was still young once the gig had finished.

It is said that the officers at Fort Campbell were on the lookout for an excuse to eject Hendrix from the ranks and their chance came when he injured his ankle in a parachute jump. Nevertheless, he left with an honourable discharge, though it's debatable he deserved it. After his discharge he relocated to our familiar location of Clarksdale while he waited for his buddy Buddy to get out of the army and join him.

He then began to hone his craft by endless touring on what was known as the Chitlin' Circuit. This consisted of venues where African American musicians could play, during a time of racial segregation. Mainly thought of as being in the South of the USA, it in fact extended to eastern and midwest cities and could even be said to include the legendary Harlem Apollo in New York. However, it's hard to imagine the chitlins from which it got its name were served somewhere like the Apollo. Chitlins, or to give it an anglicised spelling, 'chitterlings', are stewed pig's intestines, which was the house dish at many of the glorified shack clubs that staged so much great music. I don't know about you but if in a jumping club watching an ace rhythm and blues band, I've never been overcome by the raging desire for stewed pig intestines. Perhaps offal should have more of a place in rock and roll. How great perhaps to luxuriate in the glorious disco spectacle of Chic while tucking into some haslet, which is a sort of slimy pig's unspeakable-bits meatloaf. Or why not admire the stage presence and scintillating moves of Janelle Monáe while staving off hunger with a nice slab of brawn – that glorious meat jelly terrine made with the flesh from the head of a calf or hog? If you don't see it on the menu but 'head cheese' is there, then that's the same thing. So, vegetarians, if out and about on the Chitlin' Circuit don't go for the head cheese option thinking you'll be safe. Be warned. Eat before you go. Most dishes you'll find at these places will to some extent contain sweepings from the abattoir floor. My grandma used to consider tripe – the lining from a cow's stomach – and chitterlings something of a delicacy when doused in malt vinegar of a Saturday teatime as the wrestling finished and the football results came in. I preferred the boiled egg option myself as even at that tender age her plate resembled the aftermath of a sacrificial ritual in which an animal had been disembowelled – which was of course pretty much exactly what had happened.

So with the aroma of freshly fricasseed pig's intestines in his nostrils and gradually impregnating his stage clothes, Jimi Hendrix toured endlessly as guitar gun for hire with such acts as The Isley Brothers, Little Richard,

Wilson Pickett, Ike and Tina Turner, Sam Cooke and Jackie Wilson, and you're not going to construct a curriculum vitae like that unless you are at the top of your game. What Hendrix's state of mind was as he inhabited this netherworld is hard to say but there is talk of him being so flamboyant that he upstaged Little Richard on occasion, even though he was ostensibly a member of the backing band. One can only imagine the reaction backstage of diminutive Dick to the theatricality of his hired-hand guitarist. Clearly, this was already a young man with stars in his eyes and quite possibly ideas above his station. He also learned a few tricks during this period including playing guitar with his teeth, a skill he had witnessed when performed by Alphonso 'Baby Boo' Young. It seems, then, that Hendrix was absorbing everything he could on the Chitlin' Circuit to prepare him for the superstardom he felt was rightfully his.

When Hendrix arrived in London he found a music scene obsessed by the blues. The Stones, the Yardbirds, Eric Clapton and Jimmy Page were all looking for ways to stamp their own identity on the music of the Mississippi Delta. Hendrix recruited drummer Mitch Mitchell and bass player Noel Redding to create The Experience and almost immediately it became clear that a new version of the blues had been born. Jimi was of course steeped in Howlin' Wolf, Arthur 'Big Boy' Cruddup, John Lee Hooker, Elmore James, Robert Johnson, Leadbelly, Son House and Sonny Boy Williamson, so he understood the roots of the genre better than anyone in London at the time. He'd played in its homeland and had that music running through his veins. But his mission was to stretch its boundaries in a fashion comparable to John Coltrane stretching the bounds of jazz. Hendrix had a vision of journeying to the outer limits of the blues and beyond into improvisational clouds of guitar verging on white noise. It's almost as if he foresaw the shoegazing movement of the late Eighties and early Nineties when bands like My Bloody Valentine handed out earplugs to the audience to protect them from the sustained sonic assault. Certainly someone like the American composer Glenn Branca's experiments in guitar and orchestral cacophony owed a great deal to Hendrix's sonic pioneering. Not that Jimi's love of pure improvisation to express the moment made him neglect the rudiments. His girlfriend Kathy Etchingham talks of him repeating the same riff over and over again on the sofa at their flat until, with a satisfied chuckle, he finally got it right.

Hendrix also sought to redefine the sound of the rock guitar. He has been much copied but never quite equalled: you can assemble the same Marshall stacks and Fender Stratocaster, even turn it upside down and play it with your teeth if you must, but it will never be quite the same. There was a connection between Hendrix and his instrument, and the swirling volume wrapped around him that created something unique and magical. No one else could do it. He was the best in the world.

Of course, he had some help. He was not averse to trying out the latest effects, one of which was called the Octavia. It was designed by a guy called Roger Mayer, who as well as being a sonic wave engineer for the

Ministry of Defence also built electronic musical devices. Apparently the Octavia creates a double echo effect but had been dismissed by Jimmy Page as 'too far out'. There was no such thing as 'too far out' for Jimi, though. In fact Mayer was much taken with Hendrix's approach to music and his following it wherever it took him. Mayer talked about throwing a pebble in a pond and the ripples being unpredictable as they depended on how you threw the stone. This he considered to be the way Hendrix liked to work best. We're almost back to 'honour thy error as a hidden intention'. If you're headed into the unknown you are going to have to embrace the notion of chance.

In some ways Hendrix was heading into the unknown when he made his way to Woodstock. The festival was hugely overpopulated and organisation lax to say the least. Stage times for various acts drifted wildly and Hendrix ended up taking the stage at nine, some say eight, on the Monday morning of 18 August 1969. By this time a great many of the reported half a million punters had shuffled off in their blankets and headbands back to their real lives and effective sanitation, but estimates still say there were two hundred thousand there when Jimi began his two-hour set, although who was counting is hard to say. How do you look at a crowd and work out how many people are in it? Especially if you've been on acid for a week. Jimi was apparently offered a slot at midnight on the Sunday but, as festival headliner and the highest paid artist on the bill, he wanted to close proceedings. Evidently one of the organisers Michael Lang's idea had been to follow Hendrix with the singing cowboy Roy Rogers, who politely declined.

But not only did Hendrix arrive at the site not sure what time he would be going on, he wasn't exactly sure what he was going to play. With The Experience disbanded he went on stage with a new band sometimes referred to as the Band of Gypsys, though this was another trio with Billy Cox on bass and Buddy Miles on drums, but more accurately known as Gypsy Sun and Rainbows. Billy Cox was there, as was Mitch Mitchell behind the drum kit from The Experience. There were also two largely inaudible percussionists in Juma Sultan and Jerry Velez and, controversially – as why would someone as ridiculously talented as Hendrix need back-up – Larry Lee on second guitar. The band was loose and underrehearsed and certainly Mitchell had grave misgivings about their ability to gel. It must have been difficult for him after the incendiary psych-out he'd known before alongside Jimi and Noel Redding.

I won't bother giving you the full set list of that epic performance as you can easily look it up but at one point there is a medley consisting of 'Voodoo Chile', 'Purple Haze', about five minutes of solo improvisation and the American national anthem 'The Star-Spangled Banner'. It's also notable that whether by accident or design Hendrix is wearing red, white and blue. He sports a red headband, blue flared jeans and a fringed white top. Had he chosen that outfit, less garish than many of his stage outfits, just to accentuate this moment? Who knows, but performing 'The Star-Spangled Banner' was not unusual for him. In fact it is said that there are up to fifty different live recordings of it. What's interesting about this version though is that here is the biggest rock star in the world at the biggest festival in the world performing the sacred national anthem but letting it descend into swirling clouds of pure noise. What is widely read into this is that Hendrix is performing a protest song without words. Here are blissed-out hippies gathered in a field at the same time as their contemporaries are being slaughtered in Vietnam. Hendrix, who had known military service, is said to have been attempting to recreate the sounds of dive bombers, explosions and gunfire in the squalls of sound emanating from his fretboard. Jimi himself never confirmed this, preferring instead to talk in vague terms of an electrical buzz that was in the air in America at that time, but the moment has been preserved as iconic. It was a performance of a distorted, destroyed and despairing national anthem at a time of distorted reality amidst the destruction and despair of war. Al Aronowitz in the *New York Post* called it 'the single greatest moment of the Sixties'.

The Vietnam War finally ended in 1975 after twenty years of fighting. Jimi Hendrix's life ended sooner, just over a year after Woodstock on 18 September 1970 in the Samarkand Hotel in London. And the Sixties effectively ended just over four months early on 18 August 1969, when 'The Star-Spangled Banner' in its strangulated and bastardised form rang out over the emptying desolate fields of Woodstock.

25

The Beginning is the End

In 1877 Thomas Edison recorded 'Mary Had a Little Lamb' on his phonograph. It's not exactly a banging rendition, but it was thought to be the first audio recording ever made. And subsequently a version of 'Au Clair de la Lune', sung by an unidentified woman, turned up, apparently dating from 9 April 1860. It's not the most precise vocal performance you will ever hear but that is said to be down to the inability of the available tech way back then to replay at constant speed. In fact, there are those who say the vocalist is male but played at the wrong speed. Apparently, it was recorded on a device called the 'phonautograph', which used a diaphragm to respond to sound. This was then etched onto paper, utilising soot from an oil lamp. How on earth Édouard-Léon Scott de Martinville came up with this idea I have absolutely no clue, but he must have been some kind of genius for sure. And we owe him a massive debt of gratitude.

If good old Édouard-Léon hadn't initiated man's desire to record music, there might have been no Thomas Edison on the phonograph, no 1887 launch of the gramophone record by Emile Berliner, no 1906 Victrola record player introduced by RCA Victor to play discs at various speeds for the first time, no double-sided records as launched by Columbia in 1908, no first vinyl twelve-inch recording of Beethoven's Fifth Symphony by the Philadelphia Symphony Orchestra conducted by Leopold Stokowski in 1931, no first LP record in 1948's *The Voice of Frank Sinatra*, no first popular music compact disc in 1982 with ABBA's *The Visitors* (though Billy Joel's *52nd Street* hit the shops first).

And while it would scarcely constitute a major loss, this book wouldn't exist either. Okay, if de Martinville hadn't done it then I'm sure someone else would have got round to it eventually. Nevertheless, we owe so much to the pioneers of recorded sound who made the records that changed rock and roll forever. Quite a journey. And as I reflect on passing through my own momentous journey and resuming a life in music, I can only give humble thanks to all of them. Without them these sonic crossroads might have remained forever unvisited.

Acknowledgements

Many thanks to my long-time, long-suffering agent Caroline Chignell at PBJ Management and to my new-found mentor and editor at Canongate, Hannah Knowles. Cheers also to Justin Lewis for all the fine-tuning. A firm handshake to my old friends Phil Walmsley and James Whitmore who came and stood at the cross-roads with me. Much love to the girls: Bella, Holly, Mimi, Rose, Isla and Esme. Finally, eternal gratitude to Dr Lip Lee, Mr Jay Goswamy, Ged McDermott and all the rest of the amazing staff at the Christie and Wythenshawe hospitals who made me well again.